HAITIAN CREOLE PHRASEBOOK

Essential Expressions for Communicating in Haiti

Cécile Accilien, Ph.D., and Jowel C. Laguerre, Ph.D.

New York   Chicago   San Francisco   Lisbon   London   Madrid   Mexico City
Milan   New Delhi   San Juan   Seoul   Singapore   Sydney   Toronto

The McGraw·Hill Companies

Copyright © 2011 by The McGraw-Hill Companies, Inc. All rights reserved. Printed in the United States of America. Except as permitted under the United States Copyright Act of 1976, no part of this publication may be reproduced or distributed in any form or by any means, or stored in a database or retrieval system, without the prior written permission of the publisher.

3 4 5 6 7 8 9 10 11 12 13 14 15 16   QFR/QFR   1 9 8 7 6 5 4 3 2 1

ISBN   978-0-07-174920-6
MHID   0-07-174920-9

Library of Congress Cataloging-in-Publication Data

Laguerre, Jowel C. (Jowel Christian)
    Haitian Creole Phrasebook : essential expressions for communicating in Haiti
/ by Jowel C. Laguerre, Cecile Accilien.
      p.   cm.
    Includes bibliographical references and index.
    Text in English and Haitian French Creole.
    ISBN 0-07-174920-9 (alk. paper)

    PM7854.H32 L34   2010
    447'.97294—dc22   2010020197

Map created by Douglas Norgord, Geographic Techniques

Bonus Audio Download
A bonus audio recording that features selected phrases from this book can be found on mhprofessional.com. Simply follow these easy steps:
1. Go to mhprofessional.com.
2. Search for Haitian Creole Phrasebook or the book's ISBN 0071749209.
3. Locate "Downloads" beneath the book's cover image.

McGraw-Hill books are available at special quantity discounts to use as premiums and sales promotions or for use in corporate training programs. To contact a representative, please e-mail us at bulksales@mcgraw-hill.com.

This book is printed on acid-free paper.

Tèt ansanm pou bati yon Ayiti ki desantralize ak estab!
Heads together to build a decentralized and sustainable Haiti

To the memory of Roseline Massé, *fanm vanyan*, who was a caring, thoughtful, and loving rainbow in so many people's clouds and especially Cécile's.

To the memory of Sonia Biassou Lamothe, Jowel's other mother.

We dedicate this book to the memory of the many Haitians and non-Haitians who lost their lives in the earthquake of 01/12/10 and to the rebuilding of a more prosperous Ayiti Cheri!

Contents

Acknowledgments   *xi*
Introduction   *xiii*

Part I   Basic Vocabulary

Chapter I

Basics of Haitian Creole   *3*

Pronunciation   *4*
Alphabet   *8*

Chapter 2

Greetings and Introductions   *11*

Key Words and Phrases   *12*
Greetings   *13*
Introductions   *14*
Occupations   *15*
Family and Friends   *16*
Wishes   *18*
Talking on the Phone   *19*

Chapter 3

Opinions and Descriptions   *21*

The "Magic" Words   *21*
Likes and Dislikes   *22*
Preferences   *23*
Opinions   *24*
Agreement and Disagreement   *25*
Description   *25*
Colors   *27*

Chapter 4

Numbers, Time, and Weather   *29*

Cardinal Numbers   *29*
Expressions of Quantity   *32*
Ordinal Numbers   *32*
Telling Time   *33*
Days of the Week   *36*
Months of the Year   *37*
Weights and Measures   *38*
Weather   *39*

Part 2   Living and Working in Haiti

Chapter 5

Transportation and Directions   *43*

Key Words and Phrases   *44*
Asking for Directions   *45*

Modes of Transportation   *46*
Renting a Car   *49*
Around Haiti   *51*

Chapter **6**

Money, Shopping, and Services   *55*

Banking   *56*
Shopping   *57*
Buying Clothing   *60*
Pharmacy   *61*
Post Office   *62*
Internet   *63*

Chapter **7**

Accommodations   *65*

Key Words and Phrases   *66*
Checking into a Hotel   *66*
Requests and Problems   *67*
Checking Out of a Hotel   *69*
Rentals   *69*

Chapter **8**

Food and Drink   *71*

Key Words and Phrases   *72*
At a Restaurant   *73*
Beverages   *76*
Shopping for Food   *78*

Chapter 9

Security and Emergencies   *85*

Key Words and Phrases   *85*
At the Police Station   *87*
Theft and Loss   *88*
Seeking Medical Care   *89*
Borders and Visa   *90*

Part 3   Specialized Vocabulary

Chapter 10

Relief Effort   *95*

Key Words and Phrases   *96*
Talking About the Earthquake   *104*
Food   *105*
Shelter   *106*
Human Protection   *107*
Children   *108*
Women   *109*
Education   *109*

Chapter 11

Construction and Rebuilding   *111*

Key Words and Phrases   *111*
Interviewing a Potential Employee   *117*
Giving Instructions   *119*

Tools and Equipment *120*
Vehicles and Heavy Equipment *121*
In an Emergency *121*

Chapter 12

Medical Care *123*

Key Words and Phrases *124*
Asking About Pain *125*
Asking About Symptoms *126*
Illnesses *129*
Body Parts *130*
Patient Instructions *132*
Medication Instructions *132*
Women's Health *133*

Appendix A   Grammar Overview *135*
Appendix B   Verb Table *169*
English to Creole Glossary *179*
For Further Reading *201*

Acknowledgments

The idea of a Haitian Creole book started to take shape in Reno, Nevada, in 2005 at Marie-Yollens and Molière Berthoumieux's house where we (Cécile and Jowel) met. There, we discussed, analyzed, agreed, disagreed on various aspects of Haitian Creole. However, we both agreed that there was a need for more publications of texts to teach Haitian Creole. For the past five years across the two coasts and at times across two continents we have continued to work on that textbook. Then, the earthquake in Haiti hit on January 12, 2010, and the urgency and necessity to communicate during the relief effort pushed them (along with the vision of the team at McGraw-Hill and especially Karen Young) to visualize this current phrasebook. Immediately, Elmide Méléance and John Moran started looking at possibility for publishers. As the Haitian Creole proverb states: *Men anpil, chay pa lou* [With many hands, the load is not heavy]. So, we wish to say *Mèsi anpil* [Thank you very much] to the various hands that have made this project possible. We would like to give special thanks to Marie-Yollens and Molière Berthoumieux; and a special thanks to John F. Moran, New York University.

We thank the following colleagues who have helped in so many ways with their expertise and consultation to make this book possible: Eddy André (*Mèsi pou tcho-tcho yo*), faithful patriot and great Creolist; Elmide Méléance, Maryland Writing Project, Towson University; Giselle Rémy Bratcher, Columbus State University Archives. Special thanks also to colleagues in the Department of Modern & Classical Languages at Columbus State University: Alyce Cook, Mary L. Harbour, Jacqueline Konan, and Pedro Maligo.

A number of people willingly volunteered to help us test out some pronunciation rules for the phrasebook. We would like to thank the following people: Paula Adams, I. Malik Saafir, Claudia Vallejo, Judy Spencer, and A. Marie Young. Thank you also to Mathew D'Agostino, Joyce Baugher, Aladin Accilien, Emir Accilien, and Diana Pierre-Louis. Thank you to Philippe Accilien, who ignited Cécile's love and passion for Haitian culture and especially Haitian Creole. Thank you to Bryant C. Freeman and Frances Sweet, who gave Jowel the opportunity to expand his wings into higher education in the United States. Finally, we owe a debt of gratitude to Marie-Claude Laguerre (RN), who served as pro bono consultant for us for the medical section and who fed us well during the times we spent in Solano County, California, working on the first draft of this book. Thanks to the anonymous reviewers and proofreaders for their feedback; a special thanks to Anne François, Eastern University, in Pennsylvania.

Ayibobo pou ou Karen! It has been such a pleasure working with Karen Young, our editor, who patiently exchanged dozens of e-mails and many phone conversations with us. We are grateful to McGraw-Hill for its commitment to making this Phrasebook a reality in such a short period of time.

Introduction

Haitian culture is very vibrant, which is reflected in the language. Haitian Creole is a language filled with nuances, rhythms, and sounds. Many of these are reflected by common Haitian proverbs. It seems as if there is a proverb for every occasion:

Ayiti se tè glise.   *Haiti is a slippery land.*
Dèyè mòn gen mòn.   *Behind mountains are more*
                                    mountains.

These proverbs aptly say that Haiti is much more complex than meet the eyes.

History of Haiti

Haiti occupies the western one-third of the island of Hispaniola. (The Dominican Republic is in the other two-thirds.) Haiti has an area of 10,714 square miles or 27,750 square kilometers (about the size of the state of Maryland). The capital is Port-au-Prince. Before the earthquake in 2010, it was estimated that more than two million of the population lived in Port-au-Prince. Among the major cities are Cap-Haïtien, Jérémie, Les Cayes, Hinche, Gonaïves, and Jacmel. Haiti has two official languages: Haitian Creole and French. The majority of Haitians in Haiti do not speak French fluently. However, everyone speaks Creole, the national language.

When Columbus landed in the island of Hispaniola on December 6, 1492, he found a kingdom ruled by caciques, or chiefs. By the time the French arrived in the seventeenth century to take their piece of the action, the indigenous population was exterminated for the most part. The French had to import Africans as slaves from West Africa to continue their human exploitation. In the eighteenth century, Haiti was considered France's richest colony and was called "the pearl of the Antilles." Haiti fought and gained its independence in 1804 after a twelve-year battle with the French. As a result of Haiti's fight, Napoleon Bonaparte was forced to sell Louisiana to the United States of America in 1803, resulting in a major expansion. The United States did not recognize Haiti's independence until 1862. When Haiti became independent, it had to pay reparation to France. In the early twentieth century (1915–1934) the United States occupied Haiti. Through countless coups, dictatorships, brain drain, rural migration, and immigration, Haiti has leaned several times during its history but has remained the highest symbol of freedom for the world. Haiti's independence made it the only successful slave rebellion, the first black republic, and the second independent nation in the Americas. Haiti has a complex, vibrant, tumultuous, rich, and interesting history.

After gaining its independence, in 1804 the new nation changed its name from Saint Domingue to its original Taino name, Hayti, which means land of mountains. You will see various spellings for

Haiti: Hayti, Ayiti. Haiti is also known as Kiskeya or Haïti Thomas. Oftentimes, Haiti is also referred to as *Ayiti Cheri* (Dear Haiti). This is the way it is celebrated by many of its poets and musicians.

Culture

Haiti's culture (religion, food, language) is a blend of its history. This melting pot of history (from the Taino Indian, the West African, the British, the Spanish, and the French) is reflected in the architecture, cuisine, education, religion, and language. With a large number of Haitians living abroad, especially in the United States and Canada, the American influence (both in terms of language and culture) is constantly apparent in Haiti. In fact, many Haitians in Haiti have family members or know someone who is living outside of Haiti (in the United States, Canada, France, the Bahamas, Guadeloupe, and so forth). Haitians in Haiti often refer to these places as *lòt bò* (literally "on the other side").

While about 95 percent of the population is of African descent, the majority of Haitians living in Haiti (whether white, mulatto, dark-skinned, light-skinned, in-between) consider themselves Haitians. One noticeable ethnic group in Haiti is the Syrians (early twentieth-century Levantime immigrants), who are generally the commercial elite and oftentimes intermarry within their own ethnic group or the upper-class Haitian elite. Some people refer to anyone who is not Haitian as *blan* (white). The term *nèg/nègès* (literally negro/negress) is often used in Haiti and does not have a pejorative or racial connotation at all. In fact, you can be a white person and someone can call you a *ti nèg* (little negro) or *ti nègès* (little negress).

A rich person (regardless of skin complexion) can be called a *gran nèg* or *gran nègès*. It is even used as a term of endearment sometimes.

Generally Haitians have a strong sense of nationalism. You will sometimes hear people proudly defend their regions (northerners, southerners, and those from the Central Plateau). Each region boasts certain attributes that are particular to that region whether it is in terms of a dance, food, music, history, and so forth. Haiti has a long tradition of artists who have used various media to explore the rich diversity of the island and show its colors to the world. The subjects found in Haitian art vary from market scenes to food to animals to Vodou ceremonies.

Customs

Haitians celebrate January 1st as their Independence Day. It is customary for people to make *soup joumou* (squash soup). January 2nd, known as *Fèt dèzaye* or Ancestors' Day, is a day to spend with family and eat well. You could call it the Haitian Thanksgiving feast. Haitian music is known around the Caribbean, the most well-known is *Konpa*. Throughout the year different ceremonies are celebrated: baptism, communion, patronal saints, and carnival. The celebrations vary depending upon the region and city. Haitians are generally *bon vivan* or *jwisè*. People like to enjoy life, take it easy and take things as they come. It is common to have people gather around to tell stories in the forms of Krik? Krak! providing a close interaction between the storyteller and the listeners. Most Haitians can think of an older family member who used to tell *kont*, *blag*, and *devinèt* under the moon when they were children. Stories of Bouki and Malice—Ti Malice is the smart and mischievous character, while his friend Bouki is very naive and gullible—as well as *lougaou* (werewolf) are common in Haitian popular folktales.

Beliefs

The main religions are Roman Catholicism (about 55 percent), Protestantism (usually referring to all non-Catholic denomination), and Vodou (an official religion recognized by the government in 2003). It is not clear the number of people who practice Vodou. Vodou is an African-based religion as well as a way of life for many people. Haitians generally spelled the religion *Vodou* to differentiate it from the negative and pejorative "voodoo" often used in the United States to denote something obscure or bizarre. This religion and culture is reflected in Haiti's vibrant art, sculpture, language, and daily life. For many Haitians, Vodou is a life force, a *poto mitan* (a center pole), by which they try to understand Haiti's complex history, its myths, and its capacity and ability to survive in the face of adversity and to find meaning for what may often appear to be meaningless.

How to Use this Book

This book features words and phrases designed to help visitors to Haiti get around the country and communicate easily with Haitian Creole speakers. Part 1 covers important basics of Haitian Creole, from introductions and greetings to expressing numbers and time. Part 2 features vocabulary useful for visitors working in Haiti, with words and phrases for asking for directions, taking different forms of transportation, shopping and banking, arranging for accommodation, and talking about food. Part 3 contains specialized vocabulary for relief and rebuilding efforts.

With the words and phrases in this book, you can begin speaking Haitian Creole right away. But remember that practice makes perfect! To use your knowledge of Creole, you will need to use the words you have learned and build on new words. So, practice and say your Creole words and phrases often. As with any new language learner, you may be frustrated for not understanding right away, but stick with it and you will do well. This phrasebook offers a comprehensive and concise grammar to the beginning Haitian Creole speaker without it being dispersed in several chapters of the book.

Pronunciation

To use this book effectively, you will need to know how to pronounce words in Haitian Creole. In Chapter 1, you'll find easy-to-understand pronunciation guidelines and an overview of the whole alphabet with special notations for sounds you may not be used to.

Grammar and Verbs

In Appendix A there is a grammar review that gives you an overview of the simple grammar that exists in Creole. Verbs in Creole are simple because they do not change. In Appendix B there is a listing of common verbs for your reference.

Part **1**

Basic Vocabulary

Chapter **1**

Basics of Haitian Creole

Kreyòl pale, Kreyòl konprann.   *Creole is spoken, Creole is understood, (without mincing words).*

This proverb illustrates the idea that whatever the person says is understood. In other words, it means "to be absolutely clear." Of any other languages you speak or study, Haitian Creole is one of the simplest you will ever encounter. Its vocabulary is derived from many other languages, especially French and English, so some terms may sound familiar to the user of this phrasebook. The grammatical structure is simple, logical, and easily understood for the most part. Unlike French, Spanish, or some other languages, there is no gender difference to be noted among words. So there are no masculine or feminine differences to worry about. Pronouns are standard whether they are used as subjects or objects ("I" and "me," for example, are the same). Haitian Creole boasts only one irregular verb, *bay*, and verbs have one form throughout the different tenses. There are markers to differentiate the past, present, future, and so forth. The grammar review in Appendix A has a brief overview of how the language works.

Pronunciation (Pwononsyasyon)

The pronunciation of Haitian Creole is phonetic. Once you master the few intrinsic nuances based on the guide that follows, you should be able to read and write the language easily.

This is one of the easiest languages in the world to pronounce. In Haitian Creole, if you write a letter you must pronounce it; if you pronounce it, you must write it. There are no mysteriously written words. The sounds of some letters are modified by an accent grave (`). See the next section for the different pronunciations of the letter "e" with and without the accent, "o" with or without the accent, "a" with or without the accent. There is no waste of letters in this language. You could call it a "green language."

Pronunciation Differences Between Haitian Creole and English

Most letters in English sound the same in Creole. Here we illustrate some letters that are different as well as a combination of letters that may produce a different sound in English. There is only one way to say the letters, unlike in some other languages. When the use is different we note it. Please also see the complete alphabet at the end of this chapter:

ch as in show: **fache** (to be upset)
e as in *a*pe: **efreye** (scared)
è as in b*e*g: **vè** (worm or glass)
g always "hard," as in *g*ot: **g**aya: (to recover)
i as in s*ee*: **vizit** (visit)
j has no "d" sound in front: **jwe** (play)
o as in g*o*: **bo** (kiss)
ò as in j*aw*, r*aw*; **lò** (gold)
ou as in f*oo*d: **fou** (crazy)
r is *not* rolled, very soft, pronounced at back of throat: **radote**
     (to blabber)
s is always pronounced as an "s," never like a "z": **bese** (to go down)
y as in *y*oyo: **neye** (to sink)

Nasal Sounds

Nasal sounds are pronounced partially through the nose, but the "n" itself is not pronounced. There are no real English equivalents, but are close to:

an is somewhat like h*uh*!: **kan** (camp)
en as in s*i*nk : **men** (hand)
on like w*on*'t: **pon** (bridge)

   When a nasal sound is followed by a second "n" or by an "m," pronounce the nasal sound as usual, plus the "n" or "m" separately: *jenn* (young), *manm* (member).

When the letters "an," "en," or "on" are not meant to indicate a nasal sound, a grave accent (`) is placed over the vowel: *lamàn* (manna), *Amerikèn* (American woman), *bòn* (maid).

E-N and O-N Sounds

There are two instances when "en" and "on" do not follow the pattern described. In these cases the "e" and the "n" and the "o" and the "n" are pronounced as separate letters. They do not form a nasal sound. Please note that in the writing of the language, the hyphens do not appear and are used as reference here.

Here are some examples:

E-N

e-nmi (enemy)

pe-nisilin(penicillin)

me-nizye (carpenter)

me-naje (manage)

pe-nib (painful)

ante-nwa (funnel)

me-nopoz (menopause)

me-nase (threaten)

O-N

o-nè (honor)

ko-neksyon (connection)

ko-nekte (to connect)

bouto-nyè (buttonhole)

ko-nesans (knowledge)

ko-nyak (cognac)

bo-nè (early)

o-nivo (at the same level with)

-AJ and -AY Sounds

Several hundred Haitian Creole words can end interchangeably in "-aj" or "-ay." The pronunciation is phonetic and different, but it is a slight difference. Either pronunciation is understood. Thus:

Sabotaj and **sabotay**
  (sabotage)

maj and **may** (wise men)

Plaj and **play** (beach)

lonbraj and **lonbray** (shade)

esklavaj and **esklavay** (slavery)

gadinaj and **gadinay** (breeding)

plasaj and **plasay**
  (common-law mariage)

kafouyaj and **kafouyay**
  (entangle)

However, there are exceptions to this often quoted rule, where "-aj" and "-ay" are not interchangeable. Some examples:

-AJ Only

kaj (cage)

raj (rage)

naj (swimming)

saj (wise)

-AY Only

pay (straw)

tokay (namesake)

fritay (fried food)

rapyay (rabble)

-ÒJ, -ÒY, -OUJ, and -OUY Sounds

Only a small number of words ending in "-òj" also end in "-òy," "-ouj," and "-ouy." The pronunciations are different, but so are phonetic for the "j" or the "y."

fòj and **fòy** (forge)

kalòj and **kalòy** (birdcage)

senjòj and **senjòy** (var. of large centipede)

Senjòj and **Senjòy** (Saint-Georges)

alagouj and **alagouy** (randomly)

chatwouj and **chatwouy** (octopus)

koukouwouj and **koukouwouy** (lightning bug)
lawouj and **lawouy** (rust)
patwouj and **patwouy** (patrol)
fripouj and **fripouy** (crook)

-ANY, -ENY, and -ONY Sounds

Non-native speakers frequently hesitate concerning words ending in "-any," "-eny," and "-ony." It must be remembered that the final "-y" forms a separate syllable and that it is pronounced as the "y" in "year." (Be careful not to pronounce the "y" as an "i" sound; it should be a "yay" sound as in the word "kay.") Thus:

Word	Pronunciation
chany (shoeshine boy)	**chan-y**
zorany (orange)	**zoran-y**
beny (bath)	**ben-y**
peny (comb)	**pen-y**
chawony (carrion)	**chawon-y**

Alphabet (Alfabè)

Most letters in English sound the same in Creole, and there is only one way to say the letters, unlike in some other languages.

Letter		Example
a	**ay**	b*ay*
b	bee	*B*ob

c	see	*C*eline
d	dee	*D*avid
e	ay	br*a*id
f	ef	*F*rank
g	gee	*G*eorge
h	ash	*ash*
I	ee	*e*agle
j	gee	*g*iant
k	ka	*kha*ki
l	el	*l*azy
m	em	*m*orning
n	en	*en*emy
o	oh	*O*hio
p	pay	*p*oor
r	err	*r*ead
s	ess	*s*andwich
t	tee	*t*ime
v	vay	*v*ehicle
w	doob vay	*w*ater
y	igrèk	*y*oyo
z	zèd	*z*ero

Chapter 2

Greetings and Introductions

Bonjou ou se paspò ou.   *Good morning is your passport.*

The way you say "good morning" is how you will be received. In other words, courtesy will take you far.

In Haiti, people generally greet one another by saying *Bonjou* (before noon) or *Bonswa* (after noon). Friends or younger people may be less formal and they can say *Sak pase?* (What is happening?) to which the person may answer *Nap boule* (literally, "we are burning" but meaning "we are holding on"), *Nou la* (We are here), *Nap Kenbe* (We are holding on). To show respect, one may add *Mesye* (Mr.) or *Madanm* (Madam) or *Madmwazèl* (Ms. or Miss) to the greeting.

It is important to note that greeting people is very common. You do not just greet people you know. You greet everyone and everyone greets you. It is considered very impolite to arrive somewhere and not greet people. If it is a group of female and male, you may say *Bonjou Mesyedam* (Good morning, ladies and gentlemen). There is still, though, the expectation that the younger person will greet the older when they meet, and the less powerful greets the more powerful. Educated and well-behaved people don't necessarily ascribe to that, however.

Key Words and Phrases (Mo ak Fraz Kle)

Mr.	Mesye
Mrs.	Madanm
Ms.	Madmwazèl
People	Moun
Child	Timoun
Adult	Granmoun
Excuse me	Eskize mwen
Sorry	Eskize mwen
Please	Tanpri
	Souple
Thank you very much	Mèsi anpil
OK	Oke
No problem	Pa gen pwoblèm
	Pa gen pàn
God willing	Si Bondye vle
Please sit	Chita souple
I don't speak Haitian Creole.	Mwen pa pale kreyòl.
I only speak a little Haitian Creole.	Mwen degage mwen.
Can you repeat that please?	Ou kapab repete sa souple?

Can you speak more slowly?	Ou kapab pale pi dousman?
Do you speak English?	Èske ou pale anglè?

Greetings (Salitasyon)

Hello	Alo
	Bonjou
	Bonswa
Good morning, ladies and gentlemen.	Bonjou mesyedam.
How are you?	Kijan ou ye?
	Kouman ou ye?
What's up?	Sak pase?
	Sa k ap fèt?
Nothing much.	Anyen menm.
We are making progress	N ap vanse.
I am fine, thank you.	Mwen byen, mèsi.
	Mwen pa pi mal.
We are hanging in there.	N ap kenbe.
How about your family?	E moun yo?
	E fanmi an?
They are fine, thank you.	Yo byen, mèsi.
Good morning	Bonjou.
Good afternoon	Bonswa.
Good night	Bòn nwit.
Good-bye	M ale
See you later.	N a wè pita.

See you tomorrow.	N a wè demen.
See you again.	N a wè ankò.
See you next week.	N a wè lòt senmenn.

Introductions (Entwodiksyon)

What is your name?	Kijan ou rele?
	Ki non ou?
My name is Marie.	Mwen rele Mari.
What about you?	E ou menm?
I am happy to meet you.	Mwen kontan rekonèt ou.
	Mwen kontan fè konesans ou.
Where are you from?	Ki kote ou moun?
	Moun ki bò ou ye?
I am from Carrefour.	Mwen se moun Kafou.
Are you from Haiti?	Eske ou se moun Ayiti?
I am from Miami.	Mwen se moun Miyami.
I am from the United States.	Mwen se moun Etazini.
I am from Canada.	Mwen se moun Kanada.
How long are you staying here?	Konben tan w ap fè isit?
Two weeks	De senmenn
Two months	De mwa
I am here for work.	Mwen vin travay isit.
Can I offer you something to drink?	Mwen ka ba ou yon bagay pou bwè?
Yes, please.	Wi, tanpri.
What would you like to drink?	Kisa ou ta renmen bwè?
No, thanks.	Non, mèsi.

Occupations (Okipasyon)

Are you a student?	Eske ou se etidyan?
What are you studying?	Kisa w ap etidye?
I am studying . . .	M ap etidye…
business.	jesyon/biznis.
medicine.	medsin.
biology.	byoloji.
What do you do for work?	Ki travay ou fè?
I am not working.	Mwen p ap travay.
I am unemployed.	Mwen se chomè.
I am a(n) . . .	Mwen se…
teacher/professor.	pwofesè.
nurse.	enfimyè.
doctor.	doktè.
lawyer.	avoka.
mechanic.	mekanisyen.
engineer.	enjenyè.
farmer.	kiltivatè.
artist.	atis.
merchant.	machann.
baker.	boulanje.
journalist.	jounalis.
agronomist.	agwonòm.
pastor.	pastè.
priest.	pè.

Family and Friends (Lafanmi ak Zanmi)

In Haiti, family ties are very important. Family goes beyond blood relation. In many instances, you will hear people refer to someone as *matant* (aunt) or *monnonk* (uncle) even if they are not really their aunt or uncle, it is a matter of respect. You will also sometimes hear someone refer to their common-law husband or wife as their *mari* (husband) *ou madanm* (wife). There is a proverb that says *Vwazinaj se fanmi* (Neighbors are family).

Family	Fanmi
Father	Papa
Mother	Manman
Child/children	Pitit
	Timoun (Timoun means literally small person)
Daughter	Pitit fi
Son	Pitit gason
Husband	Mari
Wife	Madanm
Brother	Frè
Sister	Sè
Grandfather	Granpapa
	Granpè
Grandmother	Grann
	Granmè
Aunt	Matant
	Tant

Uncle	Monnonk
	Tonton
Niece	Nyès
Nephew	Neve
Godmother	Marenn
Godfather	Parenn
Woman	Fanm
Man	Nonm
Friend	Zanmi
Coworker	Kòlèg
Boyfriend	Mennaj/nonm
Girlfriend	Mennaj/fanm
Associate	Asosye
Boss	Patwon
	Chèf
Neighbor	Vwazinaj

Monkonpè and *Makomè* are the terms the parents and godparents used to refer to one another. This expresses a special bond.

Talking About Family and Friends (Pale de Fanmi ak Zanmi)

This is . . .	Sa a se…
This is my cousin (male).	Sa se kouzen mwen.
This is my cousin (female).	Sa se kouzin mwen.
Are you married?	Èske ou marye?
Yes, I am married.	Wi, mwen marye.

I am single.	Mwen selibatè.
She/he is engaged.	Li fiyanse.
This is my fiancé(e).	Se fiyanse mwen.
They are living together.	Yo plase.
They are divorced.	Yo divòse.
We are separated.	Nou separe/kite.
I am widowed.	Mwen vèf (Mari/Madanm mwen mouri).
Do you have children?	Èske ou gen timoun/pitit?
Yes, I have two children.	Wi, mwen gen de pitit.
Do your children go to school?	Èske pitit ou yo ale lekòl?
How many people are in your family?	Konben moun ki gen nan fanmi ou?
How many people live in the courtyard?	Konben moun ki abite nan lakou* a?
How are your parents?	Kijan papa ou ak manman ou ye?
How are your relatives?	Kijan paran ou ye?

*Note: In Haiti, many families and neighbors share a yard referred to as a *lakou*.

Wishes (Swè)

Happy Birthday!	Bòn fèt!
Merry Christmas!	Joye Nwèl!
Happy New Year!	Bòn Ane!
Congratulations!	Felisitasyon!
I congratulate you.	Mwen felisite ou.

Have a good trip!	Bon vwayaj!
Good luck!	Bòn chans!
I wish you a Happy Birthday!	Mwen swete ou bòn fèt!

Talking on the Phone (Pale nan Telefòn)

Alo!	Hello!
Who is on the line?	Kimoun ki nan telefòn lan?
	Kiyès ou ye?
It is (I) Jack.	Se mwen menm Jak.
Who would you like to speak with?	Ak kimoun ou ta renmen pale?
I would like to speak with Paul.	Mwen ta renmen pale ak Paul.
May I leave a message for Marie-Claude?	Eske mwen ka kite yon mesaj pou Mariklod?
I don't speak Creole.	Mwen pa pale kreyòl.
Do you speak English?	Èske ou pale anglè?
Can you please repeat that?	Ou kapab repete sa souple ?
Can you say that more slowly?	Ou kapab di sa a pi dousman?
May I have your phone number?	Ou kapab ban mwen nimewo telefòn ou?
My phone number is 3-432-3456.	Nimewo mwen se twa kat san trannde-trannkat senkann sis (3-432-3456).
I called you, but your phone was busy.	Mwen te rele ou, men telefòn ou te okipe.
Hang up the telephone.	Rakwoche telefòn lan.

Don't hang up the telephone.	Pa rakwoche telefòn lan.
Pick up the phone.	Pran telefòn lan.
Answer the phone.	Reponn telefòn lan.
You have the wrong number.	Ou fè yon move nimewo.
The line is busy.	Telefòn lan okipe.
I cannot hear.	Mwen pa kab tande.
This phone is not working.	Telefòn lan pap travay/mache.
I lost reception.	Mwen pèdi koneksyon.
I would like to buy a phone card.	Mwen ta renmen achte yon kat telefòn.
I would like to buy a SIM card.	Mwen ta renmen achte yon kat SIM.
How do I dial the United States?	Kijan pou mwen rele Etazini?
How do I dial Canada?	Kouman pou mwen rele Kanada?

Chapter 3

Opinions and Descriptions

Pa konnen pa janm al lajistis. *I don't know never goes to court.*

Haitians love having debates. People often get into very heated discussions especially when discussing politics or religion. When in doubt you should just say *Mwen pa konnen papa* (I do not know) or *Kisa ou menm ou panse* (What do you think?).

The "Magic" Words (Mo Majik)

Before expressing any opinions, it's important to know these essential words for showing courtesy and respect.

Please	Tanpri
	Souple
Thank you	Mèsi
Thank you very much	Mèsi anpil

You're welcome	Pa gen de kwa
	De ryen
	Ou merite
No problem	Pa gen pwoblèm
	Pa gen pàn
Excuse me	Eskize mwen
I'm sorry	Eskize mwen

Likes and Dislikes (Sa ou Renmen ak sa ou pa Renmen)

To say that you like something:

I like/I love	Mwen renmen
I really like/love	Mwen vrèman renmen
	Mwen renmen anpil
He adores	Li adore
What we like best is . . .	Sa nou pi renmen se…
What she enjoys most is . . .	Sa li pi renmen se…
You enjoyed the meal?	Ou te renmen manje a?
Their favorite meal is conch.	Manje yo pi renmen an se lanbi.
I quite like bananas.	Mwen renmen fig tout bon.

To express things you do not like:

We do not like spinach.	Nou pa renmen zepina.
He does not like fruits at all.	Li pa renmen fri ditou.

They do not like mangoes much.	Yo pa twò renmen mango.
Why do you loathe fish?	Poukisa ou pa vle wè pwason?
I am allergic to seafood.	Mwen (fè) alèji ak fridemè.

Preferences (Preferans)

To express preferences:

| I prefer | Mwen prefere |
| We would rather have water. | Nou pi pito dlo. |

To ask someone about what they like:

Do you like music?	Èske ou renmen mizik?
Does he enjoy dancing?	Èske li renmen danse?
Which one do you prefer?	Kilès/Kiyès ou pi renmen?
Which would you rather have?	Kilès ou ta prefere genyen?
Do they prefer yellow or blue?	Jòn ak ble kiyès yo pi pito?
What do you like best?	Sa ou pi pito?

To express indifference:

It doesn't matter.	Sa pa fè anyen.
It doesn't make any difference.	Sa pa fè okenn diferans.
He does not care.	Sa pa fè li anyen.
It's up to you.	Sa depan de ou menm.
She does not mind.	Sa pa deranje li.

Opinions (Opinyon)

To ask for or give an opinion:

What do you think?	Kisa ou panse?
	Sa ou panse?
I would like to know your view.	Mwen ta renmen konnen sa ou panse.
Could you give me your opinion?	Èske ou kapab ban mwen opinyon ou?
You are right.	Ou gen rezon.
We are wrong.	Nou gen tò.
They are not right.	Yo pa gen rezon.
He/she thinks that . . .	Li panse ke…
Personally, I think that . . .	Pèsonèlman mwen kwè ke…
I am sure (that) . . .	Mwen si (ke)…
	Mwen pozitif (ke)…
I am convinced (that) . . .	Mwen sèten (ke)…
In my view . . .	Daprè mwen…
They believe (that) . . .	Yo kwè (ke)…

To avoid giving your opinion or advice:

That depends.	Sa depan.
I have no opinion on this.	Mwen pa gen okenn opinyon sou sijè sa a.
I'd rather not express my opinion.	Mwen prefere pa bay opinyon mwen.
I've never thought about it.	Mwen pa janm panse de sa.

Agreement and Disagreement (Dakò ou Pa Dakò)

To agree or express approval:

What a good idea!	Ala yon bon lide!
It's a good thing!	Se yon bon bagay!
It was a good idea!	Se te yon bon lide!
I agree with you!	Mwen dakò avèk ou!
I think you are right!	Mwen panse ou gen rezon!
We support the reconstruction.	Nou sipòte rekonstriksyon an.
	Nou apiye rekonstriksyon an.
It is true (that) . . .	Se vre (ke)…

To express your disapproval or disagreement:

I can't stand being late.	Mwen pa renmen an reta.
I can't stand this guy, he is rude.	Mwen pa ka sipòte eleman sa a, li malelve.
I disagree.	Mwen pa dakò.

Description

Here are useful words you can use to describe people or things. Remember that adjectives generally follow the noun as they do in French.

Beautiful	Bèl
Big	Gwo

Small	Piti
Skinny	Mèg
	Mens
Tall	Wo
Short	Kout
Fat*	Gra
Nice	Janti
Generous	Gen kè nan men
Good	Bon
Bad	Move
Likeable	Bon moun
Helpful	Sèvyab

Marian is beautiful.	Maryàn bèl.
Joseph is tall.	Jozèf wo.
The children are helpful.	Timoun yo sèvyab.
Look at that big boy.	Gade yon gwo ti gason.
Jezila is very skinny.	Jezila chèch anpil.
Lamèsi, you are short!	Lamèsi, ou kout!
Are the mangoes sweet?	Èske mango yo dous?
Mangoes from my village are always sweet!	Mango nan peyi mwen toujou dous!

*This can be a positive description in a country where there are many skinny people.

Colors (Koulè)

Red	Wouj
Black	Nwa
Blue	Ble
Yellow	Jòn
White	Blan/blanch
Green	Vè/vèt
Brown	Mawon
Grey	Gri
Orange	Jòn abriko
Purple	Mov

What color is the car?	Ki koulè machin nan?
The car is red.	Machin nan wouj.
The lady's skirt is white.	Jip madanm nan blan.

Chapter 4

Numbers, Time, and Weather

Kay koule twonpe solèy
   men li pa twonpe lapli.

A leaky house can fool the sun,
   but it cannot fool the rain.

In other words, you can fool some of the people some of the time but you can't fool all of the people all of the time.

Cardinal Numbers (Chif Kadinal Yo)

If you know numbers in French, then all your hard work has paid off because the numbers and orders are pretty much the same in Creole. Because of the recency of literacy in Haiti, we tend to not use numbers as much as Americans and others do in certain respect such as recipes. Furthermore, we tend to estimate and use expressions like *gwo* (big or large), *anpil* (many, much), *enpe* (some, a little bit).

Numbers	**Chif**
One (1)	Youn (en)
Two (2)	De
Three (3)	Twa
Four (4)	Kat
Five (5)	Senk
Six (6)	Sis
Seven (7)	Sèt
Eight (8)	Uit
Nine (9)	Nèf
Ten (10)	Dis
Eleven (11)	Onz
Twelve (12)	Douz
Thirteen (13)	Trèz
Fourteen (14)	Katòz
Fifteen (15)	Kenz
Sixteen (16)	Sèz
Seventeen (17)	Disèt
Eighteen (18)	Dizuit
Nineteen (19)	Diznèf
Twenty (20)	Ven
Thirty (30)	Trant
Forty (40)	Karant
Fifty (50)	Senkant
Sixty (60)	Swasant
Seventy (70)	Swasanndis
Eighty (80)	Katreven
Ninety (90)	Katrevendis

To form the rest of the numbers or compound numbers, you simply add the number at the end of the multiple of ten to make one word. You are simply repeating the original numbers (2, 3, 4, and so forth). For 21, 31, 41, 51, 61, we use "e en" which means "and one." For 70s and the 90s, we use the denominations 11 (*onze*, *douze*, and follow the pattern.) It is like we are saying 60 and 11 (71), 60 and 14 (74) 80 and 12 (92) or 80 and 14 (94).

Twenty-one (21)	Venteyen
Twenty-two (22)	Vennde
Thirty-three (33)	Tranntwa
Forty-four (44)	Trannkat
Fifty-five (55)	Senkannsenk
Sixty-six (66)	Swasannsis
Seventy-seven (77)	Swasanndisèt
Eighty-eight (88)	Katrevenuit
Ninety-nine (99)	Katrevendiznèf
One hundred (100)	San
One hundred ten (110)	Sandis
One hundred twenty (120)	Sanven
Two hundred (200)	De san
Three hundred (300)	Twa san
One thousand (1,000)	Mil
Two thousand (2,000)	De mil
One million (1,000,000)	Yon milyon

Expressions of Quantity (Mo Kantite)

Here are some useful terms when you want to talk about numbers in less precise terms.

Many/A lot	Anpil
Few	Kèk
Piece	Moso/ti kal
Little	Piti
Too much	Twòp
Enough	Ase

Ordinal Numbers (Òd)

To form ordinal numbers, we generally add the term "yèm" at the end of the number. We provided the first few for you and you can use them to form further ordinal numbers. We would note that for ordinal in English that ends in first (21, 31, 41, 51, 61, 81) we use *einyèm*. Seventy-first is *swasannonzyèm* and ninety-first is *katreven onzyèm*.

Ordinal Numbers	**Òd**
First	Premye
Second	Dezyèm
Third	Twazyèm
Fourth	Katriyèm
Fifth	Senkyèm
Sixth	Sizyèm
Seventh	Setyèm

Eighth	Uityèm
Ninth	Nevyèm
Tenth	Dizyèm
Eleventh	Onzyèm
Twelfth	Douzyèm
Thirteenth	Trèzyèm
Fourteenth	Katòzyèm
Fifteenth	Kenzyèm
Sixteenth	Sèzyèm
Seventeenth	Disetyèm
Eighteenth	Dizuityèm
Nineteenth	Diznevyèm
Twentieth	Ventyèm
Twenty-first	Venteinyèm

Telling Time (Di kilè li ye)

Time is relative in Haiti. Many Haitians are notoriously late, so keep that in mind as you give and take appointments. We do not have a lot of clocks or watches to keep track of time. There is something called Haitian time and it is seldom exact. Count on it being later. Haitian time is about thirty minutes to an hour late on a good day. To ask for time we use *Kilè li ye?* (What time is it?) To answer the time we use *Li twazè* (It's three o'clock). There is a famous proverb that states *Lè ou gade nan mont ou wa wè li trèzè* (When you look at your watch, you will see that it is the thirteenth hour). In other words, it will be too late. We do not use military time in Haiti and thus the meaning of the proverb, "you will run out of time."

Numbers for Telling Time

To express time in Creole, you may use the numbers below. Except for midnight and noon, you use a modified form of the number plus "è" at the end. In French it is like *heures* and in English it is like "o'clock."

Number (O'Clock)	Creole Number	Number in Time
Midnight (12)	Douz	Minwi
One	En (In)	Inè
Two	De	Dezè
Three	Twa	Twazè
Four	Kat	Katrè
Five	Senk	Senkè
Six	Sis	Sizè
Seven	Sèt	Setè
Eight	Uit	Uitè
Nine	Nèf	Nevè
Ten	Dis	Dizè
Eleven	Onz	Onzè
Twelve (Noon)	Douz	Midi

Time of Day

A.M.	Di maten
P.M. (noon until 5:59)	De laprèmidi
P.M. (after 6:00)	Diswa
Morning	Maten

Afternoon	Aprèmidi
	Apremidi
Evening/Night	Aswè or sware
This evening/tonight	Aswè a
It's late.	Li ta.
It's early.	Li bonè.

Asking About the Time

What time is it?	Kilè li ye?
Do you know what time it is?	Ou konn kilè li ye?
It's noon.	Li midi.
It's one o'clock.	Li inè.
It's two o'clock.	Li dezè.
It's three o'clock A.M.	Li twazè dimaten.
It's three o'clock P.M.	Li twazè de laprèmidi.
It's 4:15 (four plus a quarter).	Li katrè kenz.
	Li katrè eka.
It's 5:30 (five plus a half).	Li senkè trant.
	Li senkè edmi.
It's 6:45 (six plus three quarters).	Li sizè karannsenk.
It's 6:45 (seven minus a quarter).	Li setè mwen ka.
It's 1:55 (five until two).	Li dezè mwen senk.
It's midnight.	Li minwi.
At noon (exactly)	A midi pil
	A midi presi
At 7:00 (exactly)	A setè pil
	A setè presi

35

When is it ending?	(A)kilè l ap fini?
We woke up at midnight.	Nou reveye a minwi.
They eat lunch at noon.	Yo manje dine a midi.
What time do we eat breakfast?	A kilè nou manje dejennen/ manje maten?
Work begins at exactly eight o'clock.	Travay kòmanse a uitè (8) pil.
Haitians raise the flag at 8.	Ayisyen monte drapo a 8 è.
What time do you get up?	A kilè ou leve?
What time do you sleep?	A kilè ou dòmi?
You are late.	Ou an reta.
You are on time.	Ou alè.
Don't be late.	Pa rive an reta.
Be on time.	Rive alè.

Days of the Week (Jou nan Senmenn Lan)

In Creole, the days of the week sound like the ones in French.

Monday	Lendi
Tuesday	Madi
Wednesday	Mèkredi
Thursday	Jedi
Friday	Vandredi
Saturday	Samdi
Sunday	Dimanch

What day are you arriving?	Ki jou w ap rive?
I arrive on Tuesday.	M rive madi.
What day of the week is it?	Ki jou jodi a ye?
It is Sunday.	Se dimanch.

Months of the Year (Mwa nan Ane A)

The days of the month sound like the ones in French.

January	Janvye
February	Fevriye
March	Mas
April	Avril
May	Me
June	Jen
July	Jiyè
August	Out/Dawou
September	Septanm
October	Oktòb
November	Novanm
December	Desanm

What month do you return home?	Nan ki mwa w ap tounen lakay ou?
I'm going home in March.	M ap tounen lakay an mas.
What months does it rain?	Nan ki mwa lapli tonbe?
What month were you born?	Nan ki mwa ou te fèt?

| Cécile's birthday is in February. | Cecile te fèt nan fevriye. |
| January first is Independence Day. | Premye janvye se fèt lendepandans. |

Weights and Measures (Pwa ak Mezi)

The metric system has the dominant usage in Haiti. The English system of measure may also be used. Haitians have their own measures for things as well.

Centimeter	Santimèt
Inch	Pous
Meter	Mèt
Mile	Mil
Yard (not a common measure)	Yad
Gram	Gram
Kilo	Kilogram
Kilogram	Kilogram
Kilometer	Kilomèt
Liter	Lit
Half	Mwatye
Half liter	Demi lit
Quarter	Yon ka/eka
Quarter mile	Yon ka mil
Give them thirty-two dollars.	Ba yo trannde dola.
Cayes is 70 kilometers from Port-au-Prince.	Okay swasanndis kilomèt ak Pòtoprens.

How long is it?	Ki longè li?
It's ten feet.	Li dis pye.
How far is it to the hotel?	Ki distans otèl la ye?
It's five miles.	Li sen mil.
Is it within walking distance?	Moun ka ale apye?
It's too far to walk.	Li twò lwen pou ou ale apye.
It is close.	Li pre.

Weather (Tan/Tanperati)

What's the weather like outside?	Kijan tan an ye deyò a?
It is raining.	Lapli ap tonbe.
Is it snowing?	L ap fè nèj?
It never snows in Haiti.	Li pa janm fè nèj ann Ayiti.
Is it windy?	Van ap vante?
The sun is burning hot.	Solèy la cho anpil.
They announced a hurricane.	Yo di gen yon siklòn k ap vini.
Is there a drought?	Èske gen sechrès?

Part **2**

Living and Working in Haiti

Chapter 5

Transportation and Directions

Ou konn kouri, ou pa konn kache.	*You know how to run but you do not know how to hide.*
Pye kout pran devan.	*Plan your day.*

In good times and weather, transportation in Port-au-Prince and indeed in Haiti is quite a challenge.

The notion of distance is cultural. If you want directions in Haiti, just know that some Haitians are poor directions givers. People mean well and they want to help, but at times they may not have all the information and details about how to get somewhere and will try to explain it to you anyway, which may cause even more confusion. It is best to have people accompany you to show you as opposed to telling you. We have an expression *Voye yon moun al rekonèt li* (Sending someone to nowhere).

Unless you specifically hire a taxi or a taptap, transportation is ride-share. Often people are crammed into the vehicle. That is an excellent way to meet new people.

Key Words and Phrases
(Mo Kle ak Fraz)

In Haiti, we don't rely too much on the traditional north, south, west, or east to get around. Here are some words and phrases that will help you make your way around the country.

Above	Anwo
Under/below	Anba
To the left	Agoch
To the right	Adwat
Straight ahead	Toudwat
Behind	Dèyè
In front of	Devan
Far	Lwen
Not far	Pa lwen
Close/near	Pre
North	Nò/Lenò
South	Sid
	Lesid
West	Lwès/wès
East	Lès/ès
Street	(La)ri
Avenue	Avni
Corner	Kwen
Stop light	Anba limyè (nan lari)
Stop sign	Estòp/Siy estòp
Building	Gwo kay
	Bilding

Asking for Directions (Mande Chemen)

Excuse me	Eskize m
How do I get to . . .	Kijan pou m fè pou m ale (rive)…
the bus station?	estasyon otobis?
the town center?	lavil/anba lavil?
Where is the . . .	Kote…ye?
hospital	lopital la
bank	labank la
Is it far from here?	Li lwen isit la?
Should I go . . .	Se pou m vire/ale…
south?	nan sid?
north?	nan nò?
Is the tap tap heading north?	Taptap la mete tèt nan nò (anwo)?
Did you live in the west before living in Port-au-Prince?	Ou te rete nan lwès anvan ou te rete Pòtoprens?

Asking About Distance

Haiti uses predominantly meter system of kilometers, meters, centimeters, and so forth. Miles are seldom used.

Meters	Mèt
Kilometers	Kilomèt
Miles	Mil

What is the distance between Cap Haitien and Port-au-Prince?	Koben kilomèt ki genyen ant Okap ak Pòtoprens?
There is too much distance between the poles.	Gen twò gwo distans ant poto yo.
How far do you live from here?	Ki distans ou rete de isit la?
Is it too far to walk to?	Li twò lwen pou mwen ale apye?
Is it close enough to go on foot?	Li pre ase pou mache ale?
What is next to the post office?	Kisa ki sou kote lapòs la?
The Red Cross is behind the post office.	Lakwa Wouj dèyè lapòs la.
What is in front of City Hall?	Kisa ki anfas Lakomin?
I am going to run an errand downtown.	Mwen pral fè yon komisyon lavil.

Modes of Transportation (Mòd Transpò)

There are multiple modes of transportation: tour guides, taxis, private automobiles, motorcycle, and, the most used form, taptaps. The name indicates their speed, but they are very colorful and are found throughout Port-au-Prince and the roads to Carrefour, Léogane, and other parts of the country. They have a flat fee within Port-au-Prince.

Bike	Bisiklèt
	Bekàn

Car	Machin
	Oto
Taxi	Taksi
Bus	Bis
	Otobis
Airplane	Avyon
Boat	Batiman
	Bato
	Kannòt
Tap tap	Tap tap
What mode of transportation would I use to . . .	Ki fason pou m ta fè pou…
go to Lagonav?	ale Lagonav?
go to Les Cayes?	ale Okay?
travel in Port-au-Prince?	ale yon kote nan Pòtoprens?
go to the town center?	ale lavil?
go to the hospital?	ale lopital la?
Take a fishing boat.	Pran yon kannòt.
Take a bus.	Pran yon otobis.
Take a taxi cab.	Pran yon taksi.
Go on foot.	Ale apye.
Go on motorcycle.	Ale sou motosiklèt.
	Ale sou moto.
Go on bike.	Ale sou bisiklèt.
Where is the . . .	Kote…
bus station?	estasyon bis la?
airport?	ayewopò a?
taxi stand?	estasyon taksi yo?
tap tap?	taptap la?

Buying Tickets

Transactions for transportation, except for airlines, are done with cash. You usually pay as you get off the vehicle. A few drivers may want the money ahead of time. You may request a receipt, but don't be disappointed if you do not get one. We seldom use them. For some modes of transportation, you may need to go to the station for buses travelling to the countryside. We do not tip the drivers, but if you choose to, they would appreciate it. There is no specific place for a bus or a taptap to drop you off. You ring the bell or knock on the window behind the driver to signal that you have arrived. You get off and head to the passenger's side and pay him or her.

Ticket	Biyè
One-way	Ale senp
Round-trip	Ale retou
Bus station	Estayon autobis
Train station	Estasyon tren
Airport	Ayewopò
How much is a ticket to . . .	Konbyen biyè a vann pou…
Port-au-Prince?	Pòtoprens?
the town center?	lavil la?
What is the fare?	Konbyen li koute?
I would like a one-way ticket.	Mwen ta renmen yon biyè ale senp.
I would like a round-trip ticket.	Mwen ta renmet yon biyè ale retou.

What time does the . . . leave?	Akilè … li kite?
tap tap	tap tap
bus	bis
Is it running late?	Èske li an reta?

Taking a Taxi or Tap Tap

Please take me to . . .	Mwen bezwen ale nan…
this address.	adrès sa a.
the town center.	anba lavil.
How much does it cost to	Konbyen ou mande pou mennen
go to . . .	m nan…
Port-au-Prince?	Pòtoprens?
Please slow down.	Ale pi dousman souple.
Please hurry.	Ale pi vit souple.
How much is the fare?	Konbyen li koute?
Stop here.	Rete la a.
I'll get out here.	M ap desann la a.

Renting a Car (Pou Lwe yon Machin)

Yon can rent a car at the airport in Port-au-Prince or in some limited places outside of the airport. You want to make a reservation ahead of time and ask for a car with good tires. Flat tires are common in Haiti. You can also rent a driver with the car. Driving is hazardous especially in crowded Port-au-Prince. While you must obey the rules of the road that are common to other countries, you must be vigilant and not be surprised that drivers do not completely stop at stop signs; they only slow down. One drives on the right side of the road like in the United States. The horns in the cars are used extensively, similar to some big cities like New York. Drivers are often very helpful and courteous in the midst of the chaos. Driving in Port-au-Prince is a true symbol of organized chaos but one to avoid until you get used to it. You can negotiate whether you return the car full or empty to the same place or somewhere else.

Car	Machin/vwati
Driver's license	Lisans
Gas	Gaz
Where can I rent a car?	Kote mwen kapab lwe yon machin?
I need a car for . . .	Mwen bezwen yon machin pou…
three days.	twa jou.
one week.	yon senmenn.
I need a . . .	m bezwen yon…
manual car.	machin ak chanjman vitès.
four-wheel drive car.	kat pa kat (4 × 4).
	tout teren.
	machin doub diferansyèl.
automatic car.	machin otomatik.
What is the daily rate?	Konbyen lokasyon an pa jou?
How much is insurance?	Konbyen asirans la koute?
Where can I find a gas station?	Kote m kab jwenn yon estasyon gazolin/gaz?
Fill it up, please.	Ranpli li souple.
I have a flat tire.	Mwen pran pàn kawotchou.
It is overheated.	Li chofe.
It is stuck in the mud.	Li kole nan labou.

It fell in a hole.	Li tonbe nan you twou.
Help me push it down the street.	Ede m pouse l anba lari a.
I ran out of gas.	Mwen pran pàn gaz.
I need a good mechanic.	Mwen bezwen yon bon mekanisyen.
The car will not start.	Machin lan pa kapab estat.
She hit my car.	Li frape machin mwen an.
They are in an accident.	Yo fè yon aksidan.

Around Haiti (Nan Ayiti)

Haiti is divided into ten administrative departments, which are similar to American states. Each department is further divided into cities, towns, and villages. Below are the names and the capitals:

Departments and Capitals

Department		Capital	
Ouest	Lwès	Port-au-Prince	Pòtoprens
Nord	Nò	Cap-Haïtien	Okap
Artibonite	Latibonit	Gonaïves	Gonayiv
Sud	Sid	Cayes	Kay
Centre	Sant	Hinche	Ench
Grand-Anse	Grandans	Jérémie	Jeremi
Nippes	Nip	Miragôanes	Miragwàn
Nord-Ouest	Nòdwès	Port-de-Paix	Pòdepè
Nord-Est	Nòdès	Fort Liberté	Fòlibète
Sud-Est	Sidès	Jacmel	Jakmèl

Some Common Cities and Towns

Léogane	Leyogàn
Jacmel	Jakmèl
Mirebalais	Mibalè
Cabaret	Kabarè
Carrefour	Kafou
Arcahaie	Akayè
Mariani	Maryani
Saint-Louis du sud	Senlwidisid
Saint-Louis du nord	Senlwidinò
Aquin	Aken
Titanyen	Titanyen
Belle Anse	Bèlans
Pétion-Ville	Petyonvil
Lascahobas	Laskawobas
Port-Margot	Pòmago
Bainet	Benè
Saint-Marc	Senmak

Islands

Ile de la Tortue	Latòti
Ile de la Gônave	Lagonav
Ile à Vâche	Ilavach
	Dilavach
Les Cayemites	Kayimit

Chapter 6

Money, Shopping, and Services

Milat pòv se nèg, nèg rich se milat.	*The poor mulatto is a negro, the rich negro is a mulatto.*

The currency used in Haiti is the gourdes. Oftentimes though, we talk about the dollar. Five gourdes (*goud* in Creole) is the equivalent of $1. But the exchange rate is constantly changing. It can vary from 1 U.S. dollar being equivalent to an average of 8 Haitian dollars or 40 gourdes. Because of the close proximity to the United States, sometimes there are places that will accept U.S. dollars. To be clear when you are quoted a price, make sure that it is Haitian dollars. Haiti is very much a cash economy. Very few places take credit cards. ATMs are not a common way of exchanging money. There are very few banks with ATMs. It is best to have cash.

Banking (Afè Lajan)

Money/Currency	Lajan
American dollar	Dola ameriken
Canadian dollar	Dola kanadyen
Euro	Ero
Peso (Dominican)	Peso
Cruceiro (Brazilian)	Krisero
Gourdes (Haitian)	Goud
Bank	Bank
Traveler's check	Chèk vwayaj
Personal check	Chèk pèsonèl
Black market	Mache nwa
Check	Chèk
ATM	Machin pou moun al retire lajan nan bank
Identification	Idantifikasyon
Signature	Siyati
Small change	Ti monnen piti
Teller/cashier	Kesye
How much is the exchange rate?	Konbyen kòb la ye lè ou chanje lajan?
Where is the bank, please?	Kote bank la ye souple?
I'd like to change money.	Mwen ta renmen chanje lajan.
Can I get money with my credit card?	Èske mwen ka pran lajan avèk kat kredi mwen?
Can I have money transferred here from my bank?	Èske mwen ka transfere lajan de bank mwen?
What time does the bank open?	A kilè bank la ouvè?

What time does the bank close?	A kilè bank la fèmen?
I've lost my traveler's check.	Mwen pèdi chèk vwayaj mwen.
The numbers are . . .	Nimewo yo se…
Where is an ATM?	Kote gen machin pou moun al retire lajan nan bank?

Shopping (Fè Mache)

There are several ways for people to shop in Haiti. There are indoor supermarkets as well as outdoor open-air markets. There are also merchants who station themselves at street corners or in front of schools, churches, or wherever there is traffic. Merchants also walk around carrying things that they sell. These are not regulated, but that is a common way to buy things. In some supermarkets you can get reimbursed for some items; just be aware that it is not a common practice. But you will not get reimbursed when you purchase something from the outdoor markets and from the street vendors.

Where is the . . .	Ki kote…a ye?
pharmacy?	famasi
supermarket	makèt
market (outdoor)	mache
bakery	boulanjri
butcher shop	bouchri
bookstore	libreri
I need . . .	Mwen bezwen…
groceries.	fè mache.
	pwovizyon.

clothing.	rad.
toiletries.	bagay pou fè twalèt.
	bagay pou pwòpte kò.
	bagay pou fè bèl.
How can I get to the market?	Kijan pou mwen rive nan makèt la?
What time does the market open?	Akilè makèt la ouvè?
What time does the market close?	Akilè makèt la fèmen?
Do you take credit card?	Èske ou pran kat kredi?
Do you take dollars?	Èske ou pran dola?
I would like something for . . .	Mwen ta renmen yon bagay pou…
How much is it?	Konbyen sa a koute?
I would like please . . .	Tanpri, mwen ta renmen…
I am looking for . . .	Map chache…
Do you have . . .	Èske ou genyen…
I would like more . . .	Mwen ta renmen plis…
I would like less . . .	Mwen ta renmen (pi piti)/ (mwens)…
That's enough.	Sa ase.
I'm just looking, thanks.	Mwen jis ap gade, mèsi.
Can I look at this?	Mwen ka gade sa a?
What is this?	Ki sa sa a ye?
May I have a bag?	Ou ka ban mwen yon (sak)/ (sachè)?
May I have a receipt?	Ou ka ban mwen yon resi?
It's broken.	Li kraze.
I would like a refund.	Mwen ta renmen ou remèt mwen lajan mwen.

Common Merchant Questions
(Kesyon pou Machann)

At the store, the merchant may ask you:

Can I help you?	Kijan mwen ka ede ou?
What would you like?	Kisa ou ta renmen?
Is that all?	Sa sèlman?
Is that enough?	Èske sa ase?
I do not have any at all.	Mwen pa genyen (anyen) ditou.
How many do you need?	Konbyen ou bezwen?
How much do you need?	Ki kantite ou bezwen?

Bargaining (Fè Pri)

In general, you can always bargain in Haiti except if you are in a store where the prices are already set. Bargaining is a cultural phenomenon and an opportunity for interaction between the seller (*machann nan*) and the buyer (*pratik la*). Oftentimes, the price will be inflated for anyone who does not look Haitian or who does not speak Creole. The idea of bargaining is a way for both parties to come out satisfied, so people should not be afraid to bargain.

Bargaining	Machande
	Fè Pri
Better	Pi bon
Cheap	Bon mache
Expensive	Chè
Price	Pri

How much is this/that?	Konbyen sa a koute?
I will not take it, thanks.	Mwen pap pran li mèsi.
This is very expensive.	Sa a chè anpil.
Can you give me a better price?	Ou ka ban mwen yon pi bon pri?
What is your last price?	Ki dènye pri ou?
Can you lower the price?	Ou ka bese pri a?
I will pay 200 gourdes.	Map peye desan (200) goud.
This is my last price.	Se dènye pri mwen.
Is there one that is cheaper?	Èske gen youn ki mwen chè?

Buying Clothing (Achte Rad)

People can buy clothing and toiletries items in department stores as well as in open-air market. There are also a lot of used clothing called *pèpè* or *kenedi* and they can be found in various places. They are called *kenedi* because the importation of secondhand clothing started during the Kennedy era.

Shirt	Chemiz
Pants	Pantalon
Shorts	Chòt
	Bout pantalon
Shoes	Soulye
Socks	Chosèt
Sneakers	Tenis
Sandals	Sandal
Flip flop (sandal)	Sandal plastik
	Pantouf
	Boyo

Sweater	Swètè
	Chanday
Dress	Rad
Skirt	Jip
Tie	Kòl
	Kravat
T-shirt	Mayo
Swimming suit	Kostim deben
Rain gear	Bagay pou lapli
	Poncho
	Enpèmeyab
Can I try it on?	Èske mwen ka mezire li?
It's too big.	Li twò gro.
It's too small.	Li twò piti.
Do you have one bigger?	Èske ou gen youn ki pi gwo?
Do you have one smaller?	Èske ou gen youn ki pi piti?

Pharmacy (Famasi a)

Over the counter medications can be purchased in small stores called *boutik* as well as in pharmacies. Like in the United States, the pharmacist in Haiti can give you advice for common illnesses such as cold, toothache, headache, fever, malaria, and so forth. Please note that antibiotics can be purchased without a prescription.

I need . . .	Mwen bezwen…
soap.	savon.
shampoo.	chanpou.
toothpaste.	pat.

Do you have . . .	Èske ou gen…
ibuprofen?	grenn pou doulè?
antacid?	renmèd pou zègrè?
vitamin?	vitamin?
penicillin?	penisilin?
aspirin?	aspirin?
Tylenol?	tilenòl?
	kafenòl?
antibiotics?	antibyotik?
What do you recommend for . . .	Ki sa ou rekòmande pou…
headache?	maltèt?
toothache?	maldan?
backache?	do fè mal?

Post Office (Lapòs)

Address	Adrès
Airmail	Kourye avyon
Amount	Kantite lajan
Envelope	Anvlòp
Airmail envelope	Anvlòp avyon
DHL	D(day)H(ash)L(El)
Express mail	Lèt eksprès
	Lèt rapid
Registered mail	Lèt rekòmande
Letter	Lèt
Mail	Lèt
	Kourye

Mailbox	Bwat lèt
	Bwat postal
Mailman	Faktè
Package	Pake
Postcard	Kat postal
Postage	Lajan pou tenm
Stamp(s)	Tenm
I would like to mail a letter.	Mwen ta vle poste yon lèt.
Where is the post office?	Kote lapòs la ye?
The main post office is damaged.	Gwo Biwo prensipal lapòs la kraze.
Where can I buy a stamp?	Ki kote mwen ka achte yon tenm?
How much is it?	Konbyen li ye?
I want stamps for a letter to the United States.	Mwen vle tenm pou m poste yon lèt Ozetazini.
I want to mail this letter . . .	Mwen vle voye lèt sa a...
to the United States.	Ozetazini.
to Canada.	Kanada.
to France.	Lafrans.
by express mail.	Eksprès.

Internet (Entènèt)

In Haiti, cybercafés are very common. A cybercafé can range from a place with one or two computers to twenty plus. It is a place where you can use the Internet, make international calls, send fax, make photocopies, and buy blank CDs and jump drives. The service will vary based on the specific cybercafé.

Computer	Konpitè/òdinatè
E-mail	Imèl/mèl
Internet access	Entènèt
Cybercafé	Sibè Kafe
Jump drive	Jump/Kle USB
I would like to use the computer.	Mwen ta renmen navige sou nèt la.
I want to check my e-mail.	Mwen vle tcheke imèl/mèl mwen.
How much does it cost?	Konbyen li koute?
It costs three dollars an hour.	Li koute twa dola pou chak èdtan.
How do I turn it on?	Kijan pou mwen limen li?
The screen is blank.	Ekran an vid.
Do you have telephone access on the computer?	Konpitè/Òdinatè a ka fè apèl entènasyonal?
Do you accept credit cards?	Nou pran kat kredi?
No, cash only.	Non, lajan kach sèlman.
Do you sell jump drives?	Èske ou vann jump/kle USB?
This computer does not work.	Konpitè/Òdinatè sa a pa mache.
It crashed.	Li pa mache.
	Li kraze.
The keyboard does not work.	Klavye a /Kibòd la pa mache.
I will give you another one.	Map ba ou yon lòt.
Is there another cybercafé nearby?	Èske gen yon lòt sibè kafe bò isit la?

7

Accommodations

Dòmi pa konn mizè.   *Sleep does not know misery.*
Ranje kabann ou avan dòmi   *Fix your bed before you are sleepy.*
   nan je ou.

Accommodations in Haiti can range from five-star hotels to a
simple hut or even a tent. In Haitian culture, if it is an area where
security is not an issue, people are often very generous in terms of
welcoming you to their homes. Hostels and bed and breakfasts are
not common. If you are staying with a family, more than likely
meals will be included as part of your stay. In hotels, you may want
to check to see if breakfast and other meals are included as part of
the room rate. Since the earthquake of 2010 has destroyed a large
majority of the hotels in Port-au-Prince (the capital) and Jacmel (one
of the main tourist towns in the south), if you are going to these
areas, it may be challenging to find accommodation. Carrying your
own tent is advisable.

Key Words and Phrases
(Mo Kle ak Fraz)

Address	Adrès
Hotel	Otèl
Room	Chanm
Bed	Kabann
Bathroom	Twalèt
Do you know of a good hotel?	Èske ou konnen yon bon otèl?
What is the address?	Ki adrès la?
Please write down the address.	Tanpri ekri adrès la.
Take me to the hotel please.	Mennen mwen nan otèl la tanpri.

Checking into a Hotel
(Rive Nan Otèl la)

Hello	Bonjou
	Bonswa
My name is . . .	Mwen rele…
I have a reservation.	Mwen gen yon rezèvasyon.
I do not have a reservation.	Mwen pa gen rezèvasyon.
It's for two nights.	Se pou de (2) nwit.
I would like a room . . .	Mwen ta renmen yon chanm…
with a single bed.	avèk yon sèl kabann.
with two beds.	ak de kabann.
with a double bed.	avèk yon kabann pou de moun.
with a toilet.	avèk yon twalèt.

with a shower.	avèk yon douch.
with air conditioning.	avèk è kondisyone.
How much does the room cost?	Konbyen kòb chanm nan ye?
Does it include breakfast?	Èske manje maten nan pri a?
I am staying for . . .	Map rete pou…
three nights.	twa nwit.
one week.	yon senmenn.
two weeks.	de senmenn.
It's too expensive.	Li twò chè.
Do you have a cheaper room?	Èske ou gen yon chanm ki pi bon mache?
Is there a discount for students?	Èske gen yon rabè pou etidyan?
What is the address?	Ki adrès la?
Can you write the address?	Èske ou ka ekri adrès la?
Can I see the room please?	Mwen ka wè chanm nan souple?
The room is satisfactory.	Mwen satisfè ak chanm nan.
The room is unsatisfactory.	Mwen pa satisfè ak chanm nan.

Requests and Problems (Demann ak Pwoblèm)

Do you serve . . .	Èske nou bay manje…
breakfast?	manje maten?
	dejennen?
lunch?	manje midi?
dinner?	soupe?
From what time to what time?	De kilè a kilè?
Is there a laundry?	Èske gen yon kote pou lave rad?

Is there a post office?	Èske gen lapòs?
Is there a bar?	Èske gen yon ba?
Could you wake me up at 7 A.M.?	Èske ou ka leve mwen a setè (7) di maten?
Is there a safe?	Gen yon kote mwen kapab mete bagay mwen an sekirite?
Sorry, the key is lost.	Eskize mwen, kle a pèdi.
I need another . . .	Mwen bezwen yon lòt…
blanket.	lèn.
pillow.	zòrye.
towel.	sèvyèt.
soap.	savon.
The room needs to be cleaned, please.	Chanm nan bezwen netwaye, tanpri.
The room is too hot.	Chanm nan twò cho.
There is too much noise in the room.	Chanm nan gen twòp bri.
There is no hot water in the room.	Pa gen dlo cho nan chanm lan.
There is no electricity in the room.	Pa gen kouran nan chanm lan.
The lamp does not work.	Lanp lan pa mache.
The toilet doesn't work.	Twalèt la pa mache.

Checking Out of a Hotel (Lè Wap Kite Otèl La)

Good morning	Bonjou
Good afternoon	Bonswa
I would like to check out.	Mwen ta renmen kite.
Here is the key.	Men kle a.
How much?	Konbyen kòb?
May I pay . . .	Mwen kapab peye…
with a credit card?	avèk kat kredi?
with a traveler's check?	avèk chèk vwayaj?
There is a mistake in the bill.	Gen yo erè nan bil la.
The amount is more than what I was quoted in the beginning.	Lajan plis ke sa yo te di lè mwen te antre.
May I leave my luggage here until later?	Mwen ka kite sak mwen la jiska pita?

Rentals (Lwe)

For people staying long-term, housing will more likely be handled by an agency. Generally, people rent houses or apartments for the whole year. However, in the major cities you may find someone who can rent you a room, apartment, or house for a shorter length of time (ranging from one month to six months).

I would like to rent . . .	Mwen ta renmen lwe…
a house.	yon kay.
an apartment.	yon apatman.
	yon kay.
a room.	yon chanm.

For how long?	Pou konbyen tan?
For one week.	Pou yon senmenn.
For three months.	Pou twa mwa.
For a year.	Pou yon ane.
How much does it cost?	Konbyen kòb li koute?
Is there a contract?	Èske gen yon kontra?
What is included in the house?	Kisa ki vini ak kay la?
You have to pay for electricity.	Fòk ou peye pou elektrisite.
You do not have to pay for water.	Ou pa bezwen peye pou dlo.
For the room everything is included.	Pou chanm nan tout bagay ladan li.
You are responsible for your own food.	Ou reskonsab manje ou.

Staying with Friends (Rete ak Zanmi)

Here are some ways to express appreciation when staying with friends.

Thank you for letting me stay with you.	Mèsi paske ou kite mwen rete ak ou.
I will stay for two weeks.	Mwen ap rete pou de senmenn.
I would like to contribute to the household.	Mwen ta renmen kontribye yon ti kòb pou kay la.
I appreciate your hospitality.	Mwen apresye ospitalite ou.

Chapter 8

Food and Drink

Se de dwèt ki manje kalalou.

One can only eat callalou (okra) with two fingers (because it is slippery).

If, as some say, Creole is a perfection of French, then Haitian cuisine is the perfection of the French cuisine. It is, however, more abundant in its portions and has a zip that can make you sweat. So, if you don't like spicy food, make sure to ask *pa twò pike* or *san piman* (not too hot/spicy or without pepper). The variety of the food is worth the calories. The national dish is *diri kole ak pwa* (red beans and rice). You cannot leave Haiti without tasting "rum punch" and a "prestige" beer. You should also sample the coconut milk. Our fruits, especially *mango* and *papay* (papaya), are heavenly delicious, or *koupe dwèt* (literally cut off your fingers).

Key Words and Phrases (Mo ak Fraz Kle)

Appetizers	Goute
Bar	Ba (snack ba)
Beer	Byè
Breakfast	Dejennen
	Dejene
	Manje maten
Café	Kafe
Delicious	Bon anpil/Koupe dwèt
Dinner	Soupe
Dish	Pla/asyèt
Drink (noun)	Bwason/bweson
Drink (verb)	Bwè
Expensive	Chè
Food	Manje
Street food	Aleken
	Manje kwit
Hungry	Grangou
Inexpensive	Bon mache
	Pa chè
Lunch	Dine
	Manje midi
Market	Mache
Menu	Meni
	Lis manje
Reservation	Rezèvasyon
Restaurant	Restoran

Rum	Wonm
Supper	Soupe
Thirsty	Swaf
Tip	Tip
	Poubwa
Waiter	Gason
	Sèvè
Waitress	Madanm
	Madmwazèl
Water	Dlo
Wine	Diven
I'm hungry.	Mwen grangou.
Do you know a good restaurant?	Ou konnen yon bon restoran?
Is it inexpensive?	Li bon mache?
Does it serve good Haitian food?	Yo sèvi bon manje Ayisyen?
Is there an American restaurant?	Gen yon restoran Ameriken?
Do I need to make a reservation?	Mwen bezwen rezèvasyon?

At a Restaurant (Nan Yon Restoran)

There are some excellent restaurants in Haiti that the natives must tell you about because they do not advertise. People do not eat out a lot, but young people and business people tend to do that more. Most restaurants are casual, but a few are prestigious, especially at the hotels. They are usually inexpensive, and the food is delicious. There are many street food vendors. Keep street food to a minimum because of the potential health hazard associated with the lack of current infrastructures (dust, possible dead animals, garbage, and so forth). You can tip anything you want in Haiti, and it helps the waiters/waitresses. You do not need to tip a specific percentage.

We need a table for . . .	Nou bezwen yon tab pou…
two.	de.
three.	twa.
four.	kat.
May I see a menu?	Èske mwen ka gade yon meni?
Do you have a menu in English?	Ou gen yon meni an angle?
What do you recommend?	Kisa ou kòmande?
Can you recommend a Creole dish?	Ou kab rekòmande yon pla kreyòl?
What is the specialty?	Kisa ki pi bon isit la?
What's that?	Kisa sa ye?
I would like . . .	Mwen ta renmen…
fish.	pwason.
chicken.	poul.
	poulè.
goat.	kabrit.
fried pork.	griyo.
rice.	diri.
beans.	pwa.
beans and rice.	diri kole ak pwa.
Can you bring me more . . .	Ou kab pote plis…pou mwen?
bread	pen
water	dlo
Check, please.	Kont la souple.
How much is the bill?	Konbyen nou dwe ou?

Is the tip included?	Tip ladan?
	Poubwa ladan?
The food was excellent.	Manje a te bon anpil.
I couldn't eat another bite.	Mwen pa ta kab pran pa menm yon lòt bouche.
I am full.	Vant mwen plen.
I love Creole food!	Mwen renmen manje kreyòl!

Special Requests (Demann Espesyal)

I am a vegetarian.	Mwen se vejetaryen.
Do you have dishes without meat?	Ou gen pla san vyann?
I am allergic to . . .	Mwen alèji ak…
milk.	lèt.
eggs.	ze.
peanuts.	pistach.
fish.	pwason.
shellfish.	pwason ak ekay.

Typical Haitian Dishes (Pla Tipik Ayisyen)

The typical meals in Haiti may be divided between breakfast (*dejennen*), lunch (*dine*), and dinner (*soupe*). Breakfast vary widely. A typical Haitian breakfast may include eggs (*ze*), plantain (*bannann*), banana (*fig*), watercress (*kreson*), liver (*fwa*), sweet potato (*patat*), cornmeal (*mayi moulen*), oatmeal (*avwàn*), porridge (*akasan*), and bread (*pen*). The lunch consists of a combination of the following: meat (*vyann*) or fish (*pwason*) of all kinds, rice (*diri*), fried plantain (*bannann peze*), and juice (*ji*). The dinner (*soupe*) tends to be lighter and may include some of the breakfast items. Now, as life changes, lunch and dinner may interplay. Seafood is common in Haiti. They include fish with all the bones that may be fried (*pwason fri*) or broiled with sauce (*pwason gwo sèl*). We enjoy a variety of juices from fresh fruits: *korosòl*, *kachiman*, and *papay*. (soursop, custard apple and papaya).

Fried plantain	Bannann peze
Herring	Aran
Corn-based milky gruel (like a porridge)	Akasan
(Vanilla) Extract	Esans
Fried food (sweet potato, plantain, fish, and so forth)	Fritay
Fried pork	Griyo
Thick broth (with vegetable, meat, and so forth)	Bouyon
Soup beans	Sòs pwa
Stew	Ragou

Beverages

People in Haiti do not often go out for coffee or tea. But, friends can take friends to a *ba* where they may enjoy juice, sandwiches, and so forth. The idea of coffee shop as in the United States is not common in Haiti. However, people often go to restaurant-bars (*ba resto*) to enjoy a variety of beverages including juice, soft drinks, coffee, and alcoholic drinks. Additionally, you can taste the rum made in

Haiti (*Rhum Barbancourt*, the pride of Haiti), local beer (*Prestige*), and raw rum (*Kleren*). Kleren is usually stronger than rum. Take note of drinking and driving laws and follow the legal drinking age law of the United States.

I would like . . .	Mwen ta vle...
coffee.	kafe.
coffee with milk.	kafe ak lèt.
coffee with sugar.	kafe ak sik.

Coffee is always sweet in Haiti. You may want to ask for little sugar.

Juice	Ji
Tea	Te
Tea with lemon	Te ak sitwon
Tea with sugar	Te ak sik
Milk	Lèt
Water	Dlo
Bottled water	Dlo nan boutèy
Sparkling water	Dlo kabonate
Soda	Kola
Beer	Byè
Local beer	Prestij
A glass of white wine	Yon vè diven blan
A glass of red wine	Yon vè diven wouj
A bottle of wine	Yon boutèy diven
A drink with . . .	Yon bwason ak...
rum/rum punch.	wonm (wonm ponch).
whiskey.	wiski.

Shopping for Food (Ale nan Mache pou Achte Manje)

Because of the economic situation in Haiti, people tend to cook and eat at home. Many may have a maid (*bòn*) in their home because it is fairly inexpensive. There are good restaurants with excellent food. There are also merchants who sell food in the streets. Keep street food to a minimum because of the potential health hazard.

There are two or three ways to get food to cook: a supermarket similar to the ones in developed countries, the open market (*mache*), and along the streets. It all depends on how much money you want to spend. Here are some expressions for the taking.

Tell me where the food market is.	Ki kote mache a ye.
I want to buy . . .	Mwen vle achte…
meat.	vyann.
fish.	pwason.
bread.	pen.
vegetables.	legim.
That's enough.	Sa ase.
That's too much.	Se twòp.
More, please.	Plis, souple.
Less, please.	Mwens, souple.
I would like one kilo.	Mwen ta vle yon kilo.

Meat (Vyann)

Bacon	Vyann kochon
	Bekonn
Chicken	Poul
	Poulè
Duck	Kanna
Ham	Janbon
Turkey	Kòdenn
Egg	Ze
Beef	Bèf
Pork	Kochon
Lamb	Mouton
Liver	Fwa
Sausage	Sosis
Steak	Biftèk

Fish and Seafood (Pwason ak Fridemè)

Fish	Pwason
Catfish	Pwason manchèt
Lobster	Woma
Shrimp	Chèvrèt
Oysters	Zwit
Salmon	Somon
Seafood	Fridemè
Shellfish	Pwason (ak) ekay
Snapper	Pwason woz
Tuna	Sadin

Vegetables (Legim)

Avocado	Zaboka
Beans	Pwa
Beets	Bètrav
	Bètwouj
Cabbage	Chou
Carrots	Kawòt
Cauliflower	Chouflè
Corn	Mayi
Cucumber	Konkonm
Eggplant	Berejèn
Garlic	Lay
Green beans	Pwa tann
Green onion	Powo
Lettuce	Leti
Mushrooms	Djondjon
Onions	Zonyon
Parsley	Pèsi
Peppers	Piman
Hot pepper	Piman bouk
Plaintain	Bannann
Potatoes	Pòmdetè
Spinach	Epina
	Zepina
Squash	Joumou
Tomatoes	Tomat

Fruits (Fri/Fui)

Apples	Ponm
Apricots	Zabriko
Banana	Fig mi
Cantaloupe	Kantaloup
Grapes	Rezen
Lemons	Sitwon (jòn/vèt)
Limes	Sitwon (vèt)
Orange	Zorany
Peaches	Pèch
Pears	Pwa
Watermelons	Melon

Grains and Legumes (Grenn Tankou Pwa, Mayi, etc., ak Legim)

Corn	Mayi
Rice	Diri
Millet	Pitimi
Wheat	Ble
Beans	Pwa
Lentils	Lantiy

Dairy Products (Pwodwi ak Lèt)

Butter	Bè
Cheese	Fwomaj
Ice cream	Krèm
Milk	Lèt

| Cream | Krèm |
| Yogurt | Yawou |

Sweets (Bagay Dous)

Brittle	Tablèt
Cake	Gato
Ice Cream	Krèm (glase)
Pie	Tat
Pastry	Patisri
Sweet bread	Pen dous

Spices and Condiments (Epis)

Cinnamon	Kanèl
Clove	Jiwòf
Ginger	Jenjanm
Hot pepper	Piman pike
Oil	Lwil
Salt	Sèl
Sugar	Sik
Vinegar	Vinèg

Cooking Methods (Fason ou Kwit Manje)

Baked	Kwit
Boil	Bouyi
Grilled	Griye
Fried	Fri
Roasted	Boukannen

Kitchen Utensils (Veso Kizin)

Bowl	Bòl
Cup	Tas
Fork	Fouchèt
Glass	Vè
Kitchen	Kizin
Knife	Kouto
Matches	Alimèt
Plate, dish	Plat/asyèt
Spoon	Kiyè
Tray	Kabare

Measuring Recipes (Mezire Resèt)

When giving a recipe or asking for recipe, beware of the cultural aspect of measure. Haitians tend to use words for measures as opposed to numbers. Below is a list of words that are often used to specify small or large quantities:

A little bit	Yon ti kal
	Yon ti zwit
	Yon ti pense
A lot	Anpil
A little bit (used especially for dry food such as flour or salt)	Yon ti priz
A bit	Ti moso/Ti kal
A drop (used for liquid)	Yon gout

Chapter *9*

Security and Emergencies

Mache sou pinga ou pou pa pile   *Be cautious of the unknown.*
   "Si m te konnen."

In the years before the 2010 earthquake there were some incidents of kidnapping and violence in Haiti, especially in Port-au-Prince. The situation had calmed down and there was relative peace and security prior to the earthquake.

Key Words and Phrases (Mo Kle ak Fraz)

Security	Sekirite
Demonstration	Demonstrasyon
Hostile demonstration	Demonstrasyon malouk
Military demonstration	Demonstrasyon militè
Peaceful demonstration	Demonstrasyon trankil
Barbed wire	Fildefè

Crowd	Foul moun
Injured	Blese
Killed	Touye
	Mouri
Peace	Lapè
Rioting	Pwotestasyon
	Revandikasyon
War	Lagè
Disorder	Dezòd
Sabotage	Zak malfèktè
	Sabotaj
Mobilize	Mobilize
Risk	Risk
Strike	Grèv
Dangerous	Danjere
Security police	Polis pou sekirite
Shot	Kout zam
	Tire
Shotgun	Fizi
Shot	Tire
Threat	Menas
	Dezafi
Traffic	Sikilasyon
	Anbouteyaj
Trafficking	Trafik
	Kontrebann
U.S. aid	Èd Ameriken
Workers	Travayè
	Ouvriye

Don't shoot!	Pa tire!
Help	Ede
Political party	Pati politik
Soldier	Sòlda
	Jandam
Weapon	Zam

At the Police Station (Nan Lapolis)

Where is the police station?	Kote biwo lapolis la ye?
Does anyone speak English?	Èske gen okenn moun ki pale angle?
My colleague is missing.	Nou pa wè kòlèg mwen an.
This is her/his picture.	Men foto li.
She/He is tall.	Li wo.
She/He is short.	Li kout.
She has . . . hair	Li gen cheve…
brown	mawon.
black	nwa.
blonde	jòn.
red	wouj.
She has . . . eyes	Li gen je…
green	vèt.
blue	ble.
brown	mawon.
We haven't seen her in two days.	Nou pa wè li depi de jou.
We think she has been kidnapped.	Nou panse yo kidnape li.
Can I use the telephone?	Mwen ka sèvi ak telefòn nan?

I need to contact the . . . Embassy.	Mwen bezwen kontakte anbasad...
American	Ameriken an.
Canadian	Kanadyen.
Brazilian	Brezilyen.
Mexican	Meksiken.
British	Anglè.
Australian	Ostralyen.
Please fill out this paper.	Tanpri ranpli fòm sa a.
It is in French.	Li an franse.
Do you speak French?	Èske ou pale franse?
I understand a little bit.	Mwen konprann yon ti kras.
I will get someone to help you.	Map chache yon moun pou ede ou.
Thank you very much.	Mèsi anpil.

Theft and Loss (Vòl ak Pèt)

Somebody stole my wallet.	Yon moun vòlò bous mwen.
What was in it?	Kisa Ki te ladan li?
There was money.	Te gen lajan ladan l.
Someone broke into my car.	Yon moun kase machin mwen an.
I need a police report for my insurance policy.	Mwen bezwen yon rapò polis pou mwen bay asirans mwen an.
I have lost . . .	Mwen pèdi...
my airline ticket.	tikè avyon mwen.
my passport.	paspò mwen.
my car key.	kle machin mwen.

my watch.	mont mwen.
my bag.	valiz mwen.
driver's license.	lisans mwen.
credit card.	kat kredi mwen.
laptop.	konpitè/òdinatè.
	laptòp mwen.
passport.	paspò.
Where were they?	Ki kote yo te ye?
They were in the car.	Yo te nan machin lan.
They were in my room.	Yo te nan chanm mwen an.
What should I do?	Kisa pou mwen fè?
Go to the police.	Ale lapolis.

Seeking Medical Care (Chache swen Medikal)

Here are some common words and phrases that are useful when seeking medical care.

I need a doctor.	Mwen bezwen yon doktè.
I need to go to the hospital.	Mwen bezwen ale lopital.
It's important.	Li enpòtan.
Is there a doctor who speaks English?	Èske gen yon doktè ki pale angle?
Here are some common complaints.	Men kèk soufrans òdinè.
I don't feel well.	Mwen pa santi m byen.
It hurts here.	Li fè m mal la a.

My whole body hurts.	Tout kòm ap fè m mal.
I feel weak.	Mwen santi m fèb.
I feel dizzy.	Mwen santi tèt mwen ap vire.
I am hungry.	Mwen grangou.
I am thirsty.	Mwen swaf.
I feel sick.	Mwen santi m malad.
I have a . . .	Mwen…
cold.	gripe.
headache.	gen yon tèt fèmal.
fever.	gen lafyèv.
sore throat.	malgòj.

Borders and Visa (Fwontyè ak Viza)

Agency	Ajans
Army	Lame
Border	Fwontyè
Borderland	Teritwa ki sou fwontyè
Border crossing	Travèse
	Janbe fwontyè
Checkpoint/crosspoint	Pòs kontwòl
Boundary/boundaries	Fwontyè
	Bòn
	Limit
	Lizyè
Ministry of Defense	Ministè Ladefans
Officer	Ofisye
Order	Lòd

Prison	Prizon
Speed/speeding	Vitès
Speed up	Akselere
	Fè vitès
Speed bump	Polis Kouche
Bump	Chòk
	Frape
	Pouse
Bumper	Defans (oto)
Bumped into	Teke
	Kontre bab pou bab
Visa	Viza
Stop!	Kanpe!
	Rete!
Search	Fouye
	Chache
United Nations	Nasyonzini

Getting a Visa

I would like to get a visa.	Mwen ta renmen gen yon viza.
Where should I go?	Ki kote mwen dwe ale?
Where can I renew my visa?	Ki kote mwen ka renouvle viza mwen an?
Here is my passport.	Men paspò mwen.
Here are my documents.	Men papye/pyès mwen.
How much are the fees?	Konbyen kòb pou m peye?
I am staying at Hotel . . .	Mwen rete nan otèl…
Here is the address.	Men adrès la.

At a Checkpoint (Nan yon Pòs Kontwòl)

Slowdown, there is a checkpoint.	Ralanti gen yon pòs kontwòl.
Stop the car!	Kanpe machin lan!
There are soldiers with weapons.	Gen sòlda ak zam.
	Gen jandam ak zam.
How are you today?	Kijan ou ye jodi a?
May I see your driver's license and passport?	Mwen ka wè lisans ou ak paspò ou?
What are you doing in Haiti?	Kisa w ap fè Ayiti?
I am working with . . .	M ap travay avèk…
the United Nations.	Nasyonzini.
a humanitarian agency.	yon ajans imanitè.
Where are you going?	Ki kote ou prale?
I am going to Port-Margot.	Mwen prale Pòmago.
I want to search the car.	Mwen vle fouye machin nan.
Do you want me to open the trunk?	Ou vle mwen ouvè kòf la?

Part 3

Specialized Vocabulary

Chapter **10**

Relief Effort

**Lavi a se yon boul k ap woule
ou pa konnen kote l ap rete.**

*Life is like a rolling ball, you don't
know when it will be stopping.*

In the aftermath of the January 12, 2010, earthquake, a massive relief effort took place in Haiti. The relief effort covered a variety of areas: food, shelter, security, and so forth. This effort will need to continue for many years so that the infrastructure of the country, especially in Port-au-Prince, can be re-imagined. There are special economic, familial, educational, nutritional, and cultural issues that need to be addressed to help the country get back on its feet.

Being such a resilient and creative people, it is not surprising that the Haitian people have already come up with their own word to describe the earthquake of 2010. It is an onomatopoeia, *goudougou-dougoudou*. As you pronounce this word out loud, it echoes some of the sounds that many people heard during the earthquake.

Key Words and Phrases
(Mo ak Fraz Kle)

Affect	Afekte
Aftershocks	Sekous apre tranbleman
Aftermath	Konsekans
	Annaprè
Amputate	Koupe
Amputee	Moun yo koupe pati kò li
	Demanbre yon pati nan kò li
Anaesthesists	Anestezis (Moun ki bay anestezi)
Appeals	Apèl
	Fè apèl
Building code	Regleman pou bati kay
Building design	Plan pou bati
Bury	Antere
Camp	Kan
Catastrophe	Katastwòf
Catastrophic	Katastwòf
	Boulvèsan
Collapse	Tonbe
	Kraze
	Ekoule
Comfort	Konfò
Concerns	Pwoblèm
	Deranjman
Concrete	Beton
Confusion	Konfizyon
	Dezòd

Coordinate efforts	Efò òganize
	Efò tèt ansanm
Cope (with)	Lite
	Debat
	Debwouye
Corpses	Kò
	Mò
	Kadav
Corruption	Magouy
Crack (in a building)	Fele
	Fisire
	Fann
Crooked (person)	Magouyè
Crooked (not straight)	Kwochi
Damage	Dega
Death	Lanmò
Death toll	Bilan lanmò
	Kantite moun ki mouri
Debris	Fatra
	Dechè
Decomposition	Dekonpozisyon
Decomposed	Dekonpoze
Demolish	Efondre
	Detwi
	Demoli
	Demantibile
	Dekonstonbre

Deploy	Deplwòye
	Distribiye
	Mete efò
	Montre
Destroy	Kraze
	Brize
	Detwi
Destruction	Destriksyon
Devastate (destroy)	Devaste
	Sakaje
	Ravaje
	Depatcha
Dispatch	Voye
	Ekspedye
	Distribiye
Displaced	Deplase
	Moun ki oblije kite kay yo
	Moun ki oblije kite peyi yo
Doctors Without Borders	Medsen San Fwontyè
Doomed to forget	Manje bliye
Dump truck	Kamyon fatra
	Kamyon dechaj
Earthquake	Tranbleman
	Tranblemanntè
	Goudougoudougoudou
Earth-moving machines	Machin pou transpòte tè
	Machin pou fouye tè
Emergency drill	Egzèsis ijans
	Egzèsis pou moun aprann jan pou yo evakye

Emergency plan	Plan ijans
	Plan pou preparasyon lè gen ijans
	Plan pou preparasyon lè gen gwo ka
Emergency preparedness	Preparasyon pou ijans
Emergency/survival kits	Twouso èd medikal
	Twouso èd medikal ijans
	Twouso èd medikal gwo ka
Epicenter	Nannan tranbleman tè a
	Episant
Escape plan	Plan pou sove
	Plan pou evakye
Evacuation	Evakyasyon
	Chape poul
Fear	Pè
	Laperèz
First aid	Premye sekou
First responders	Swen
Food distribution	Bay
	Distribiye manje
	Sinistre
Foreign aid	Èd etranje
Frustration	Fristrasyon
	Fache
	Move
	Fristre
Fund-raising	Maraton
	Kolekte lajan

Gender	Sèks (moun nan)
	Si se fi osinon gason
Gender-based violence	Vyolans baze sou si moun nan fi
	ou gason
Hamper	Anpeche
	Jennen
Heavy-lifting machinery	Machin pwa lou
Homeless	San kay
	Moun ki pa gen kote pou yo rete
	Moun ki rete nan lari a
	Sanzabri
Humanitarian aid	Èd imanitè
Hunger	Grangou
In conjunction with	Ansanm avèk
	Ansanm ansanm
Incident control center	Katye jeneral evenman
Infrastructure	Enfrastrikti
International Red Cross	Lakwa Wouj Entènasyonal
Launch	Koumanse
	Lanse
Leak (v.)	Koule
Leak (n.)	Twou
Looting	Piyay
	Vòlè
Magnitude (earthquake)	Fòs
	Pwisans
	Fòs tranblemanntè
Makeshift camp/house	Kan refijye/tantvil

Mass graves	Fòs komin
	Mozole
	Chanyè
Massive	Gwo anpil
	Fò anpil
	Pwa senkant
Morgues	Mòg
	Nan glas
National Assembly	Palman nasyonal
	Asanble nasyonal
Natural disaster	Katastwòf natirèl
Non-governmental organization (NGO)	Òganizasyon ki pa afilye ak gouvènman (ONG)
Odor	Odè
Outpouring	Yon pakèt
	Yon bann
	Yon dividad
Pledge	Angajman
	Pwomèt
	Pwomès
Presidential Palace	Palè prezidansyèl
	Kay pèp la
Prioritize	Plase an premye
	Bay plis enpòtans
Prioritization	Premye plas
	Bay plis enpòtans
Pull out	Retire
	Sòti
	Rale

Rebuild	Rebati
	Rekonstri
Record (n.)	Rapò
Record (v.)	Bay rapò
	Anrejistre
Red Cross	Lakwa Wouj
Refugee	Refijye
Relief	Sekou
	Èd
	Soulajman
Relief effort	Efò pou ede
	Sekoure
	Soulaje
Relief operation	Aranjman pou bay moun sekou
Reporter	Jounalis
Rescue	Libere
	Sove
	Pote sekou
Resources	Resous
	Èd
Restoration	Repare
	Ranje
	Remodle
Richter scale	Echel Richtè
Rubble	Fatra
	Debri
	Dekonm
Scream	Rele
	Rèl

Seaport	Waf
Search	Chache
Search and rescue	Chache ak sove
Search and rescue mission	Misyon pou chache ak jwenn moun
Seismic activity	Aktivite tranbleman
Services	Sèvis
Sniffing dog	Chen (kap santi) fouyapòt
Stink	Move odè
Suddenly	Bridsoukou
	Avan ou bat je ou
Surgeon	Chirijyen
Survive	Rete vivan
	Sove
Telethon	Teleton: mande lajan nan televizyon oubyen telefòn
Temporary work space	Espas pwovizwa pou travay
The missing	Moun ki pèdi
	Disparèt
Trafficker	Trafikan
Trapped	Kwense
Trauma	Chòk
	Twoma
	Chòk-sou-chòk
Tremors	Sekous
	Tranbleman
Tsunami	Sounami
Unaccompanied children	Timoun ki pou kont yo
UNICEF	INISEF

United Nations Stabilization Mission in Haiti	(MINUSTAH) Misyon Nasyonzini pou Estabilizazyon Ayiti
United States Geological Survey	Gwoup ki fè ankèt jeyolojik Ozetazini
Unrest	Ajitasyon
Victim	Viktim
Wounded	Blese

Talking About the Earthquake (Pou Pale de Tranblemanntè A)

Where were you when the earthquake took place?	Ki kote ou te ye lè tranbleman an te pase?
Were you at home?	Èske ou te lakay?
Were you outside?	Ou te nan lari?
What did you hear?	Ki sa ou te tande?
I heard . . .	Mwen te tande…
Describe the noise.	Esplike jan bri a te ye?
Was it loud?	Bri a te fò?
What did you do?	Ki sa ou te fè?
What is the first thing that went through your mind?	Ki premye bagay ki te vin nan tèt ou?
How did you feel immediately after the earthquake hit?	Kijan ou te santi ou touswit aprè tranbleman an?
How do you feel now?	Kijan ou santi ou kounye a?
What happens when you hear noise?	Kisa ki rive lè ou tande bri?

Does it cause you trauma?	Èske li ba ou chòk (twoma)?
How long did you spend before you were rescued?	Konbyen tan ou te pase avan yo te sove ou?
How is the situation after the quake?	Kijan sitiyasyon an ye aprè tranbleman an?
How is your family?	Kijan fanmi ou ye?
Do you and your family get aid?	Èske ou menm ak fanmi ou jwenn èd?
What type of aid do you need?	Ki jan/Ki kalite de èd ou bezwen?
What do you need?	Kisa ou bezwen?
Besides giving monetary donation, how can our organization help . . .	Anplis ke fè don lajan, ki lòt fason òganizasyon nou an ka ede...
you?	ou?
your family?	fanmi ou?
your house	lakay ou ?
your organization?	òganizasyon ou an?
your school?	lekòl ou a?
your church?	legliz ou a?

Food (Manje)

Has your community received any food aid?	Èske nou resevwa manje nan kominote nou an?
Who is responsible for food distribution in your area?	Ki moun ki responsab pou bay manje nan zòn ou a?

Does your school have a food program?	Èske lekòl ou a gen yon pwogram manje?
Do you have money to buy food?	Ou gen lajan pou achte manje?
Are the food distributors asking people for money?	Èske moun kay distribiye manje yo ap mande moun lajan?
Do not give any money for the free food you should receive.	Pa bay moun lajan pou manje moun dwe resevwa gratis.
You need not have sex with people for free food.	Ou pa oblije kite moun fè bagay ak ou pou manje ou dwe resevwa gratis.

Shelter (Kote pou Pare Solèy)

Tents	Tant
Temporary living arrangement	Kay tanporè
	Kay pou yon ti bout tan
Shelter community: male and female	Kan refijye: pou gason ak fi
Shelter community for women and children	Kan refijye pou fanm ak timoun
Physical layout	Chema
Community-based protection	Pwoteksyon kominote a bay
Privacy of family unit	Chanm prive pou fanmi
Common area for children to play	Lakou pou timoun jwe
Distribution of shelter materials	Distribiye materyo pou fè kay
Space for community center	Espas pou sant kominotè
Space for women and girls	Espas separe pou fanm ak tifi
Do you have a place to sleep?	Ou gen kote pou ou dòmi?
Do you have a tent?	Ou gen yon tant?

Do you have land to build a house?	Ou gen tè pou bati kay?
What problems do you have with your tents?	Ki pwoblèm ou gen ak tant ou yo?
Do you have a lack of lighting?	Ou manke limyè?
Is your tent dry?	Èske tant ou a sèk?
Pay equal attention to men and women.	Bay gason kou fanm menm konsiderasyon.
The toilets are locked.	Pòt latrin yo klete.
There is a partition between families.	Gen yon separasyon ant kay chak fanmi.
Are there security concerns?	Èske nous anti nou an sekirite?
We will inspect the communal shelter.	N a enspekte kay kominotè a.
We will design and allot plotter sites.	Nou pral fè plan ak bay teren pou bati.

Human Protection (Pwoteksyon Moun)

Do you see any human abuse?	Èske ou wè moun ap fè lòt moun abi?
Are people able to express their needs?	Èske moun ka di sa yo bezwen?
Are there people who bully others?	Èske gen moun ki ap fè lòt moun pase mizè?
	Èske gen moun ki ap fè lòt moun pase tray?
	Èske gen moun ki ap fè Lwijanboje sou moun?

Are people forced to do things against their will?	Èske gen moun ke yo fòse fè sa yo pa vle?
Everyone has the right to receive free food and water.	Tout moun gen dwa pou resevwa manje ak dlo gratis.
Do not give up your children to others for food.	Pa boukante/twoke timoun ou yo pou manje.
Link humanitarian services	Fè tout òganizasyon imanitè kowòdone sèvis yo

Children (Timoun)

Make sure children have areas to play.	Asire timoun yo gen teren ak lakou pou yo jwe.
Hold schools for young children.	Fè lekòl pou jenn timoun yo.
Don't give your children to others.	Pa fè moun kado pitit ou yo.
Don't keep your children out of school.	Pa kite timoun yo pa ale lekòl.
Keep children, particularly those at the primary school level, in school.	Voye timoun yo lekòl, sitou sa ki lekòl primè yo.
What help do you need for your children?	Ki kalite sipò ou bezwen pou timoun ou yo?
Are the children sick?	Timoun yo malad?
Have you taken your sick children to the doctor's?	Ou mennen timoun ki malad yo kay doktè?
Take your child to the hospital.	Mennen pitit ou a lopital.

Women (Fanm)

Provide enough food for women to care for themselves.	Bay medam yo ase pwovizyon pou yo ka okipe tèt yo.
Make sure women are not exploited.	Fè tout sa nou kapab pou yo pa eksplwate fanm yo.
Do you face pressure from men who should give you free food or services?	Èske gen gason k ap mete presyon sou ou pou manje ak sèvis yo dwe ba ou gratis?
You need not let anyone abuse you for services.	Pa kite okenn moun fè ou enjistis pou sèvis yo.
Report abuse to the authorities.	Rapòte tout abi ak enjistis bay chèf yo.
Do not give your children away for help.	Pa bay okenn moun timoun ou yo pou yo ba ou yon ti kichòy.

Education (Edikasyon)

Link food distribution to school attendance.	Bay sinistre (manje) pou fanmi ki gen timoun lekòl.
Monitor drop-out through assistance.	Ede timoun rete lekòl ak sipò.
See if and why children and adolescents are leaving school.	Chache konnen poukisa timoun ak jenn moun ap kite lekòl.

If children are dropping out of school . . .

Si timoun ap kite lekòl…

because of lack of food.

paske yo pa jwenn manje.

provide school feeding.

mete kantin nan lekòl yo.

Provide facilities for recreation and games.

Bay teren ak kote pou timoun yo jwe ak amize you.

Ensure both boys and girls have equal access to education.

Fè sa ou kapab pou asire ke tifi gen menm opòtinite ak ti gason nan edikasyon.

Chapter **11**

Construction and Rebuilding

Men anpil chay pa lou.   *Many hands make the load lighter.*

To rebuild Haiti after the 2010 earthquake, one of the most famous of Haitian proverbs, *"Men anpil, chay pa lou,"* is especially relevant. As people from all corners of the world pour into Haiti to help with the rebuilding process, we know Haiti will once again become the "Pearl of the Antilles." For this to happen, Ayiti needs to be rebuilt in a sustainable and decentralized manner. As the cry goes, *"Alaso!"* (Onward!)

Key Words and Phrases (Mo ak Fraz Kle)

Agronomist   Agwonòm
Attention   Atansyon
Boots   Bòt

Build (v.)	Bati
	Konstwi
Brick	Brik
Bricklayer	Mason
Bucket	Bokit
Budget	Bidjè
Building	Bilding
Building code	Kòd konstriksyon
	Regleman pou bati kay
Bulb	Anpoul
Bulldozer	Bouldozè
Bureaucracy	Biwokrasi
Burn	Boule
Cable	Fil
	Kab
Careful (be)	Fè atansyon
Carpenter	Chapant
	Chapantye
Cash	Kach
	Lajan likid
Cement	Siman
Cement (to)	Simante
Cement mixer	Malaksè siman
Check	Chèk
Clean	Netwaye, pwòp
Cleanup	Netwayaj
Close	Fèmen
Cold	Frèt
Concrete	Beton

Construction	Konstriksyon
Construction materials	Materyo konstriksyon
Construction site	Chantye
Continue	Kontinye
Danger	Danje
Dig	Fouye
Dirt	Tè
Ditchdigger	Moun ki konn fouye twou
Door	Pòt
Ear protector	Pwotèj pou zòrèy
Electricity	Kouran
	Elektrisite
Electrician	Elektrisyen
Engineer	Enjenyè
Equipment	Ekipman
Eye protector	Pwotèj pou je
Fan	Vantilatè
Generator	Jeneratè
	Dèlko
Gloves	Gan
Heavy	Lou
Heavy equipment operator	Operatè machin pwa lou
Hot	Cho
House	Kay
Hurt	Blese
In advance	Davans
	Annavans
Job	Djòb
	Travay

Late	Reta
Land	Tè
	Teren
Landscape	Peyizaj
Landscaper	Jadinye
Light	Limyè
Mask	Mas
Measure	Mezire
Mechanic	Mekanisyen
Money (American)	Lajan Ameriken
Money (Haitian)	Lajan Ayisyen
Motor	Motè
Open	Ouvri
Paint (n.)	Penti
Per day	Pa jou
Per hour	Pa èdtan
	Pa è
Per month	Pa mwa
Per week	Pa senmenn
Plastic	Plastik
Plumber	Plonbye
Plumb line	Filapon
Project	Pwojè
Protection	Pwoteksyon
Protective equipment	Ekipman pou pwoteksyon
Punctual	Ponktyèl
	Alè
Remove	Retire

Road	Wout
Roadwork	Travay wout
Roadway	Wout
	Chemen
Rock	Wòch
	Galèt
Roof	Do kay
Roofer	Moun ki konn fè do kay
Room	Chanm
	Sal
	Pyès
Room and board	Pansyon
Salary	Salè
Sand	Sab
Show	Montre
Shovel	Pèl
Stop	Estòp
	Sispann
Start	Koumanse
Tape	Riban
	Riban kolan
Tape measure	Santimèt
Task	Reskonsabilite/responsabilite
	Travay
Task force	Ekip espesyal
Tax	Taks
	Enpo

Technician	Teknisyen
Temperature	Tanperati
Tile setters	Moun ki konn mete
	Poze mozayik
Tool	Zouti
Tool shed	Depo zouti
Touch	Touche
Tractor	Traktè
Truck	Kamyon
Truck drivers	Chofè kamyon
Urgent	Ijan
Vest (orange)	Vès (zabriko)
Wait	Tann
Wind	Van
Window	Fenèt
Woodworker	Ebenis
	Menizye
Work	Travay
Worker	Travayè
Workers (skilled)	Bon bòs

Indoor Work (*Travay Andedan/Alenteryè*)

Kitchen	Kizin
Bathroom	Twalèt
Living room	Salon
Dining room	Salamanje
Bedroom	Chanm

| Hall | Koulwa |
| Wall | Mi |

Outdoor Work (Travay Deyò)

Bridge	Pon
Dump	Depo fatra
Highway	Wout nasyonal
Office	Biwo
Road	Wout
Sidewalk	Twotwa
Street	Lari
Warehouse	Depo

Interviewing a Potential Employee

What is your name?	Kijan ou rele?
Where are you from?	Moun ki kote ou ye?
Where do you live?	Ki kote ou rete?
Where did you work before?	Ki kote ou te travay anvan?
What kind of work did you do?	Ki jan de travay ou te fè avan?
Do you have experience in . . .	Èske ou gen eksperyans nan...
construction?	konstriksyon?
	batiman?
welding?	soudi?
plumbing?	plonbye?
electricity?	elektrisite?
scaffold?	echafoday?

Do you have any reference?	Eske ou gen moun ki kab pale nou de travay ou?
How can I contact this person?	Kijan pou mwen kontakte moun sa a?
You are hired.	Ou jwenn travay la.
When can you start working?	Kilè ou kab koumanse travay?
Can you work every day?	Ou kab travay chak jou?
Which day you cannot work?	Ki jou ou pa kapab travay?
The salary is . . .	Salè a se…
100 dollars per week.	san dola pa senmenn.
400 dollars per month.	katsan dola pa mwa.
It is in Haitian dollars.	Se an dola ayisyen.
It is in American Dollar (green dollar)?	Dola ayisyen ou ameriken (dola vèt)?
How much for the completed job?	Konbyen pou tout travay la fini nèt?
I will pay you when you finish the job.	M ap peye ou lè ou fin fè travay la nèt.
Call me if you cannot come.	Rele mwen si ou pa kapab vini.
In an emergency, call me at . . .	Si gen yon ijans rele mwen nan nimewo…
Tell me if you have a problem.	Di mwen si ou gen yon pwoblèm.
Tell me if you don't understand.	Di m si ou pa konprann.

Giving Instructions (Bay Lòd)

Here are some commands that you can use to make requests and give instructions at the construction site.

Please hand me the . . .	Tanpri lonje…lan/an ban mwen
hammer.	mato
screwdriver.	tounvis
Put it over there.	Mete li lòt bò a.
Put it over here.	Mete li la a.
Help me lift that.	Ede mwen leve sa a.
Help her with that.	Ede li ak sa a.
Show me where you put it.	Montre mwen kote ou mete li.
Do it like this.	Fè li konsa.
Don't do it like that.	Pa fè li konsa.
Use this tool.	Sèvi ak zouti sa.
Do not use this product.	Pa itilize pwodwi sa a.
Leave it like that.	Kite li konsa.
Turn it again.	Vire li ankò.
Mix this.	Melanje sa a.
Pick this up for me.	Pran sa a ban mwen.
Turn on the lights.	Limen limyè a.
Turn off the lights.	Etenn limyè a.
Open the door.	Ouvè pòt la.
Close the door.	Fèmen pòt la.
Check the oil.	Tcheke lwil la.
Check the battery.	Tcheke batri a.

I need . . .	Mwen bezwen...
a flashlight.	yon flach.
a brush.	yon bwòs.
a ladder.	yon echèl.

Tools and Equipment (Zouti ak Ekipman)

Bolt	Boulon
Bucket	Bokit
Bulldozer	Bouldozè
Burner	Recho
Broiler	Fou
Brush	Bwòs
Cable	Fil kab
Cement mixer	Malaksè siman
Circuit breaker	Switch santral
Compactor	Konpaktè
Compressor	Konpresè
Flashlight	Flach
Forklift	Traktè pou leve chaj
Hammer	Mato
Heater	Chofaj
Ladder	Echèl
Nail	Klou
Saw	Si
Scale	Echèl
Scraper	Gratwa

Screw	Vis
Screwdriver	Tounvis
Tool box	Bwat zouti
Valve	Val/soupap
Vent	Griyaj

Vehicles and Heavy Equipment (Kamyon ak Machin Pwa Lou)

Be alert.	Rete veyatif.
	Fè anpil atansyon.
Light weight	Pwa lejè
Heavy weight	Pwa lou
Do not smoke.	Pa fimen.
Do not drink.	Pa bwè.
Do not use drugs.	Pa pran dwòg.
In case of an accident	Sizoka ta gen yon aksidan
Stop immediately.	Kanpe bridsoukou.
Turn off the engine.	Touye/tenyen motè a.
Ask for help.	Mande sekou/ Rele anmwe.

In an Emergency (Si Gen yon Ijans)

In an emergency, say "help."	Lè gen yon bagay grav ki rive rele "anmwey sekou/ede mwen."
Call the supervisor.	Rele bòs la.
	Patwon an.
Look for me.	Chache mwen.

Don't move.	Pa bouje.
	Pa brannen.
Remain calm.	Rete trankil.
	Tèt poze.
Stay with her/him.	Rete ak li.
We're giving you first aid.	Nap ba ou premye swen.
We're taking you to a doctor.	Nap mennen ou kay doktè.
Please answer my questions.	Tanpri reponn kesyon m yo.
What happened?	Kisa ki pase ?
Where did it happen?	Ki kote sa te rive?
Is anyone else inside?	Èske gen lòt moun andedan an?
What hurts?	Kisa ki fè ou mal?
Where does it hurt?	Ki kote li fè ou mal?

Chapter 12

Medical Care

Pa gen maladi ki pa gen remèd.   *Every illness has a remedy.*

Medical issues in Haiti are simple and complicated. Because of the lack of medical facilities, people tend to be deprived of healthcare and shy away from physician's care. People tend to rely heavily on folk remedies, beliefs, traditional healers, prayers, and faith. It is important that these factors be considered and respected when treating a patient. The simplicity also comes in the fact that many Haitians have faith in a Supreme healer and believe that they can be healed. It is complicated because it is sometimes hard for some non-physician or healthcare worker to appreciate these subtleties.

Mental health issues often go unnoticed or are left to the family to deal with. When treating a Haitian patient, be aware that because of their respect for medical personnel, some may agree with your assessment even if they do not understand certain orders or treatment plans. It is important to know what other medicine they may be taking and whether they were prescribed by a physician or if they are using someone else's medication.

Key Words and Phrases (Mo ak Fraz Kle)

Antibiotic	Antibyotik
Clinic	Klinik
Dispensary	Dispansè
Doctor	Doktè
	Dòk
Doctor's office	Kay doktè
Examination	Konsiltasyon
	Egzamen
Feel	Touche
	Santi
Fever	Lafyèv
Hospital	Lopital
Lab	Laboratwa
Lab test	Tès laboratwa
Medicine	Remèd
Nurse	Mis
	Enfimyè
Pain	Doulè
Painkiller	Remèd doulè
Patient	Malad
	Pasyan

Pediatrician	Pedyat
	Doktè timoun
Pill	Grenn (remèd)
Psychiatry	Sant sikatri
Shot	Vaksen
Touch	Manyen
Treatment	Tretman
X-ray	Radyografi

Asking About Pain (Konsilte sou Doulè)

How are you feeling?	Kijan ou santi ou?
What's hurting?	Kisa kap fè ou mal?
Touch where you are hurting.	Manyen kote kap fè ou mal la.
Is the pain . . .	Èske doulè a…
severe?	fò anpil?
mild?	pa twò fò?
sharp?	pike?
dull?	ansoudin?
throbbing?	ap bat?
burning?	boule?
How did the pain start?	Kijan doulè a te kòmanse?
When did the pain start?	Kilè doulè a kòmanse?
Did the pain start suddenly?	Èske doulè kòmanse toudenkou?
Is the pain stable in one spot?	Èske doulè a rete menm kote a?
Does the pain come and go or does it stay put?	Doulè a vini epi li ale oubyen èske li rete nèt?
Do you feel like one side of your body is numb (sign of stroke)?	Èske ou santi yon bò kou ou mouri?

Asking About Symptoms (Konsilte sou Sentòm [Sa ou Santi])

What's wrong, sir?	Kisa ou gen, mesye?
What's wrong, ma'am?	Kisa ou genyen, madanm?
When did this problem start?	Kilè pwoblèm sa a koumanse?
Do you urinate often?	Èske ou pipi souvan?
Do you have stomach ache?	Ou gen vant fè mal?
Do you have gas?	Ou gen gaz?
Do you have a fever?	Ou gen lafyèv?
Do you vomit?	Ou vonmi?
Are you nauseated?	Ou gen kè plen?
Are you menstruating?	Ou gen règ ou?
Are you depressed?	Ou santi ou kagou?
Are you discouraged?	Ou santi ou dekouraje?
Do you feel lethargic?	Ou gen kò lage?
Are you suicidal?	Ou santi ou anvi touye tèt ou?
Did you sprain your foot (ankle)?	Ou foule pye (je pye) ou?
Did you fall?	Ou te tonbe?
Do you have a cough?	Èske w ap touse?
Are you throwing up blood?	Ou rann (touse/tous) san?
Is your cough dry?	Ou touse sèk?
Do you sweat in your sleep?	Èske ou swe nan dòmi?
Is your chest hurting?	Lestomak (pwatrin) ou fè ou mal?
Is your . . . hurting?	Èske…ou fè ou mal?
stomach	vant
leg	janm
head	tèt

Your . . . is broken.	...ou kase.
foot	Pye
finger	Dwèt
arm	Bra
hand	Men
Did you sleep well?	Èske ou te dòmi byen?
	Ou te pase yon bòn nwit?
Do you sleep well?	Ou dòmi byen?

Common Symptoms (De sa Moun Plenyen)

Abnormal breathing	Soufle anlè
Blisters	Glòb (dlo)
Blood in the feces	San nan poupou
Blood in the urine	San nan pipi
Burning sensation	Santi boule
Bruises	Grafouyen
	Kòche
Chills	San frèt
	Chofrèt
Cold	Grip
Constipation	Konstipasyon
Cough, dry	Touse sèk
Cough, wet	Touse flèm (rim)
Cramp	Kranp
Cramping	Santi kranp
	Frison
Deafness	Soud

Dehydration	Dezidrate
	Pèdi dlo
Depression	Chagren
	Depresyon
Diaper rash	Chofi
Diarrhea	Djare
	Dyare
Discharge (secretion)	Matyè
	Sòs
Discharge (from treatment)	Egzeyate
Dizziness	Tèt vire
Dry skin	Po blanch
Edema	Anfleman
Fever	Lafyèv
Heartburn	Kè brile
Indigestion	Gonfleman
	Endijesyon
Itchiness	Gratèl
Loss of appetite	Pèd apeti
Loss of balance	Klopi klopan
Loss of consciousness	Endispozisyon
Lose consciousness	Endispoze
Lump	Boul
	Grenn
Nausea	Kè plen
Numbness	Angoudisman
Palpitations	Batman kè
Redness	(Mak) Wouj
Sore throat	Gòj fèmal

Swelling	Anflamasyon
Shortness of breath	Etoufman
Tingling	Pikòtman
Tremor	Tranbleman
Twitch	Latranblad
	Iritasyon
Vertigo	Toudisman
Vomiting	Vomisman
Weakness	Feblès
Wheezing	Souf anlè/ral

Illnesses (Maladi)

Arthritis	Rimatis
Asthma	Opresyon
Blood pressure, high	Tansyon wo
Blood pressure, low	Tansyon ba
Cancer	Kansè
Diabetes	Dyabèt
Epilepsy	Malkadi
Heart attack	Kriz kadyak
Heart disease	Maladi Kè
High cholesterol	Kolestewòl (grès nan san)
Kidney disease	Maladi ren
Liver disease	Maladi fwa
Malaria	Malarya
Malnutrition	Malnitrisyon
Stroke	Kriz tansyon

Tetanus	Tetanòs
Tuberculosis	Tibèkiloz
Typhoid	Tifoyid
Ulcers	Ilsè
UTI (**urinary track infection**)	Enfeksyon nan pipi

Body Parts (Pati nan Kò)

Ankle	Je pye
Arm	Bra
Armpit	Anba bra
Back	Do
Bone	Zo
Breast	Tete
	Sen
Buttocks	Dèyè
Chin	Manton
Ear	Zòrèy
Ear lobe	Fèy zòrèy
Elbow	Koud bra
Eye	Je
Finger	Dwèt
Foot	Pye
Gums	Jansiv
Heel	Talon
Hip	Tay
	Senti
	Ranch

Kidney	Ren
Knee	Jenou
Knee cap	Kòkòn jenou
Leg	Janm (jarèt)
Lip	Po bouch
Lower abdomen	Anba tivant
Mouth	Bouch
Neck	Kou
Nose	Nen
Nostril	Twou nen
Pelvis	Zo
	Basen
Penis	Pijon
Rib	Kòt
	Kòtlèt
Shoulder	Zepòl
Stomach (abdomen)	Vant
Thigh	Kwis
Throat	Gòj
	Gòjèt
Toe	Zòtèy
Tooth (Teeth)	Dan
Vagina	Bouboun
	Koko
	Bòbòt
	Pati fi
Wrist	Ponyèt

Patient Instructions (Lòd Doktè)

Open your mouth.	Ouvri bouch ou.
Open your mouth and stick out your tongue.	Ouvri bouch ou epi pouse lang ou deyò.
Cough.	Touse.
Take a deep breath.	Respire fò.
Inhale deeply.	Rale souf ou.
Take off your clothes.	Retire rad ou.
Lie down.	Kouche.
Touch where it hurts.	Manyen kote ki fè ou mal la.
Stand up.	Kanpe.
Get dressed.	Mete rad sou ou.
The result will be in tomorrow.	Rezilta a ap pare demen.
The result will be in later.	Rezilta a ap pare pita.
The result will be in in two days.	Rezilta a ap pare nan de jou.
Do you want a pain killer?	Ou vle yon grenn pou doulè?

Medication Instructions

Take it . . . times a day.	Pran li…fwa pa jou.
one	yon
two	de
Take the medicine before bedtime.	Pran renmèd la anvan w al dòmi.
Take it with food.	Pran li ak manje.
Take it on an empty stomach.	Pran li san manje.

Common Medications (Medikaman Komen)

Analgesic	Grenn pou doulè
Antacid	Renmèd pou asid
Antibiotic	Antibyotik
Antihistimine	Kont alèji
Aspirin	Aspirin
Codeine	Kodeyin
Cortisone	Kòtizòn
Estrogen	Estwojèn
	Òmòn fi
Insulin	Ensilin
Laxative	Medsin (renmèd pou lache)
Penicillin	Penisilin
Sedative	Kalman

Women's Health (Sante Fi)

Are you pregnant?	Èske ou ansent?
When is the baby due?	Ki dat bebe a sipoze fèt?
It is important to take care of yourself during pregnancy.	Ou dwe pran swen tèt ou byen lè ou ansent.
How many times have you been pregnant?	Sa fè konbyen fwa ou ansent.
How many children do you have?	Konbyen timoun ou genyen?
Do you breast feed them?	Ou bay timoun yo tete?
Have you ever been pregnant?	Ou te janm ansent?
What is the date of your last period?	Ki dènye dat ou te gen règ ou?

You are . . . weeks pregnant.	Ou ansent depi…senmenn.
six	sis
ten	dis
Have you had any bleeding?	Ou te konn senyen nan jou ki pase yo?
Do you breastfeed your baby?	Ou bay pitit ou a tete?
Are you using birth control now?	Èske w ap fè planin?
Do you use . . .	Èske ou sèvi ak…
the pill?	grenn planin?
the diaphragm?	kapòt pou fanm?
an IUD?	esterilè?
condoms?	kapòt?
the rhythm method?	metòd natirèl
	metòd Ojino
abstinence?	rete san fè bagay?
How long have you used this method?	Depi kilè w ap sèvi ak metòd sa a?

Grammar Overview

If you have the basic working knowledge of English, Haitian grammar will be very easy for you. If you do not, you will enjoy it and it will be clear. The grammar is quite simple. There are few exceptions, and the verb tenses are easy to remember. We advise that you use the grammar as a guide and come back to it when you are confused or when you want to impress your listeners.

Personal Pronouns (Pwonon Pèsonèl)

In Haitian Creole there are only five personal pronoun forms.

I. The First Person Singular **Mwen**

Mwen expresses all forms of the first person singular: "I," "my," "me." It also has a short form: *M*.

Mwen **Nouyòk.**	*I* am in New York.
Mwen **wè ou.**	*I* see you.

   Or

M **wè ou.**	*I* see you.
Tab *mwen* **an wouj.**	*My* table is red.
Liv *mwen* **an ble.**	*My* book is blue.
Machin *mwen* **an kraze.**	*My* car is damaged.
Ou wè *mwen***.**	You see *me*.
Ou wè *m***.**	You see *me*.
Ou ban *m* **liv la.**	You give *me* the book.
Ou pale ak *mwen***.**	You talk with *me*.

2. The Second Person Singular **Ou**

Ou expresses all forms of the second person singular: you, your. There are no problems with there being a familiar form (such as the French *tu*) or a more formal form (such as the French *vous*). If you are speaking to just one person, it is always simply *ou*. There is no short form for this pronoun, except before or after a vowel when a *w* is sometimes used in place of *ou*.

Ou **Miyami.**	*You* are in Miami.
Ou **ale lavil.**	*You* go to town.

Ou bouke.	*You* are tired.
Liv *ou* a nwa?	*Your* book is black?
Tab *ou* a vèt, wi.	*Your* table is certainly green.
Mwen ba *ou* machin lan.	I give *you* the car.
Yo wè *ou*.	They see *you*.
M ale ak *ou*.	I go with *you*.
Mwen renmen *ou*.	I love *you*.

3. The Third Person Singular Li

Li expresses all forms of the third person singular: "he," "she," "it"; "his," "her," "its," "him." It also has a short form *L*.

Li Pòtoprens.	*He* (*She* or *It*) is in Port-au-Prince.
Li ale lavil.	*He* (*She* or *It*) goes to town.

Or

L ale lavil.	*He* (*She* or *It*) goes to town.
Tab *li* mawon.	*His* (*Her* or *Its*) table is brown.
Liv *li* vèt.	*His* (*Her* or *Its*) book is green.
Machin *li* sal.	*His* (*Her* or *Its*) car is dirty.
Ou wè *li*.	You see *him* (*her* or *it*).

Or

Ou wè *l*.	You see *him* (*her* or *it*).
M ba *li* mango a.	I give *him* (*her* or *it*) the mango.

4. The First Person Plural and Second Person Plural **Nou**

Nou expresses all forms of the first person plural: "we," "our," "us." It also has a short form: *N*.

Nou Okap.	*We* are in Cap-Haïtien.
Nou bliye sa.	*We* forget that.
Nou pwòp.	*We* are clean.
Liv *nou* an jòn.	*Our* book is yellow.
Tab *nou* an blan.	*Our* table is white.
Machin *nou* an piti.	*Our* car is small.
Ou bliye *nou*.	You forget *us*.
Li pale ak *nou*.	He (She or It) talks with *us*.
Li ban *nou* chen an.	He (She or It) gives *us* the dog.

Nou also expresses all forms of the second person plural: "you" (plural), "your" (plural). It also has a short form: *N*. This is the only pronoun form likely to cause difficulty since it also expresses the first person plural: "we," "our," "us." Only from the context can its meaning be understood.

Ki jan *nou* ye?	How are *you (all)*?
Nou bliye liv la.	*You (all)* forget the book.
Nou chita deja.	*You (all)* are sitting down already.
Tab *nou* an gri.	*Your* table is gray.
Liv *nou* an jòn abriko.	*Your* book is orange.
Chen *nou* an chita.	*Your* dog is sitting down.
Mwen gade *nou*.	I look at *you (all)*.
Jan bliye *nou*.	John forgets *you (all)*.

5. The Third Personal Plural Yo

Yo expresses all forms of the third person plural: they, their, the, its short form is *Y*.

Yo pa malad.	*They* are not sick.
Yo chache chapo a.	*They* look for the hat.
Yo rive.	*They* arrive.
Kay *yo a* boule nèt.	*Their* house is completely burned down.
Kabann *yo* a piti.	*Their* bed is small.
Jaden *yo* a sèk.	*Their* field is very dry.
Li gade *yo*.	He/She/It looks at *them*.
Mwen pale ak *yo*.	I talk with *them*.
Ou ba *yo* liv la.	You give *them* the book.

Articles

The rules for articles such as "a/an" or "the" are relatively simple in Creole. They do not change and are similar to English in that sense. Please pay attention to how they are used before (a/an) and after (the).

Indefinite Articles

Indefinite articles do not present a problem for English speakers. They are placed before the noun, **just as in English**, and have only one form, *yon*.

yon chapo	*a* hat
yon chat	*a* cat
yon istwa	*a* story
yon ze	*an* egg
yon fanm	*a* woman
yon eskiz	*an* excuse
yon ougan	*a* Vodou priest
yon manbo	*a* Vodou priestess
yon egzanp	*an* example
yon timoun	*a* child

Definite Articles

Unlike indefinite articles, the definite articles require some more thinking. They have four forms in the singular and are placed after the noun. The form used depends on the ending of the word preceding it. (Note however this is far easier than in languages where the gender must be memorized for each noun or where there may be multiple exceptions!)

The basic rule here is sometimes referred to as the mirror principle: the form of the definite article used reflects the preceding word.

I. The Definite Article A

If the preceding word ends in a vowel, the form consisting of a vowel (*a*) is used:

Egzanp (examples):

dlo *a*	*the* water
dife *a*	*the* fire
lakou *a*	*the* yard
flè *a*	*the* flower
ti bebe *a*	*the* baby
mayi *a*	*the* corn
pyebwa *a*	*the* tree
lanmè *a*	*the* sea
lari *a*	*the* street
pwofesè *a*	*the* professor

2. The Definite Article La

If the preceding word ends in a consonant, the form beginning with a consonant (*la*) is used:

malèt *la*	*the* suitcase
solèy *la*	*the* sun
plaj *la*	*the* beach
fig *la*	*the* banana
legliz *la*	*the* church
lanp *la*	*the* lamp
lekòl *la*	*the* school
goud *la*	*the* gourde (Haitian currency)
bourik *la*	*the* donkey
elèv *la*	*the* student

3. *The Definite Article* An

If the preceding word ends in a nasal sound ("an," "en," "on"), the form consisting of a nasal sound ("an") is used:

lajan *an*	*the* money
avyon *an*	*the* airplane
ban *an*	*the* bench
kamyon *an*	*the* truck
batiman *an*	*the* boat
kochon *an*	*the* pig
marengwen *an*	*the* mosquito
kreyon *an*	*the* pencil
panyen *an*	*the* basket
pwason *an*	*the* fish

An is also used after the *nou* or *mou* or a word ending in *nou* or *mou*.

4. *The Definite Articles* Lan *and* Nan

If the preceding word ends in "-n" or "-m" sounds (*àn, in, òn, èn, èm, òm, oun*), the form beginning with an "n-" or "l-" is used. *Lan* and *nan* are used interchangeably as definite articles:

fanm *lan*	*the* woman
kann *lan*	*the* sugar cane
granmoun *lan*	*the* adult

machin *lan*	*the* car
timoun *lan*	*the* child
kabann *lan*	*the* bed
mòn *nan*	*the* mountain
janm *nan*	*the* leg
tenm *nan*	*the* stamp
lanm *nan*	*the* ocean wave
karèm *nan*	*the* lent
pòm *nan*	*the* apple
flèm *nan*	*the* phlegm
lèn *nan*	*the* comforter

Singular and Plural

As a general rule (meaning there are a few exceptions!), Haitian Creole words—noun, adjective, or verb—have only one form. For example, plural nouns do not take an "s" or any other marker as in English, and adjectives do not change form to agree with the noun they modify, as in French. Nor do verbs change form. Thus the general rule in Haitian Creole is: one word, one form. A really efficient language!

There is no general indicator in Haitian Creole for the plural of *yon* ("a," "an"). Just as in English the plural indicator is not expressed. Thus:

Mwen wè yon kay.	I see a house.
Mwen wè kay.	I see houses.

The plural **la, lan,** or **nan** is **yo** and is placed after the noun. Remember the spelling of the noun that becomes plural does not change:

Mwen wè kay yo.   I see the houses.

In other words, the plural corresponds to the usage in English except that there is no "s" at the end of the word in Haitian Creole. Note: *Yo* has only one form, regardless of the ending of the word immediately preceding it.

Verbs (Vèb Yo)

Haitian verbs are simple and perhaps one of the simplest among languages. Verbs are not conjugated; rather the different tenses have different markers.

The Verb To Be

Perhaps the easiest verb to learn in Creole is "to be." Usually, it is simply not expressed:

Mwen bouke.	I am tired.
Ou entèlijan!	You are intelligent!
Li pa entèlijan!	He/She/It is not intelligent!
Nou okipe.	We are busy.
Nou pa okipe.	You (plural) are not busy.
Yo bouke.	They are tired.

For emphasis, however, there are two additional forms meaning "to be." The first is with **ye**, which is used normally at the end of a question:

Kijan ou *ye?*	How *are* you?
Kisa li *ye*?	What *is* it?
Ki kote li *ye*?	Where *is* it?

Another way to express "to be" is *se*, which is used only at the beginning of a sentence or clause:

Se **vre.**	*It's* true.
Se **Fani ki grangou.**	*It's* Fanny who's hungry.
Se **anwo/anlè/sou tab la.**	*It's* on the table.

And for special emphasis, both *se* and *ye* are used in the same sentence:

Se **ameriken m** *ye.*	I *am* American
Se **Naso li** *ye.*	It's in Nassau that he *is*.
Se **ki kote li** *ye*?	Where *is* he/she it?

The Present Tense (Tan Prezan)

The present tense is expressed by the verb alone:

Mwen ede ou.	I help you.
Jan bliye sa.	John forgets that.
Yo kwè Janklod.	They believe Jean-Claude.
Mari wè tab la.	Mary sees the table.
Nou pale kreyòl.	We/You (plural) speak Creole.

The Present Progressive Tense
(Tan Prezan Pwogresif)

The present progressive tense (the "be +-ing" form in English) is expressed by the marker *ap* plus the verb:

Mwen *ap* ede ou.	I *am helping* you.

Or

M *ap ede* ou.	*I'm helping* you.
Mari *ap chante*.	Mary *is singing*.
Ou *ap pale* angle.	You *are speaking* English.

Or

Ou *ap pale* angle.	You're *speaking* English.
Jan *ap bliye* istwa a.	John *is forgetting* the story.

The Past Tense (Tan Pase)

The past tense is expressed by the marker *te* plus the verb:

Mwen *te ede* ou.	I *helped* you.
Jan *te pale* panyòl.	John *spoke* Spanish.
Nou *te wè* ou yè.	We *saw* you yesterday.
Yo te *pèdi* liv la.	They *lost* the book.
Mari *te bliye* jounal la.	Mary *forgot* the newspaper.

The Past Progressive Tense (Tan Pase Pwogresif)

The past progressive (the "was-ing" form in English) is expressed by the marker *t ap* plus the verb. *T ap* is the contraction of *te + ap*:

Mwen *t ap ede* **ou.**	I *was helping* you.

Or

M *t ap ede* **ou.**	I *was helping* you.
Mari *t ap chante.*	Mary *was singing.*
Ou *t ap pale* **angle.**	You *were speaking* English.
Jan *t ap bliye* **istwa a.**	John *was forgetting* the story.

The Future Tense (Tan Fiti)

The future tense is expressed by *a* plus the verb

Jan *a wè* **nou demen.**	John *will see* us/you (pl.) tomorrow.
Mary *a fè* **sa pita.**	Mary *will do* that later.
M kwè Anri *a bliye* **yo.**	I believe Henry *will forget* them.
Li *a gade* **sa nan de jou.**	He *will look* at that in two days.

Or

L *a gade* **sa nan de jou.**	He'*ll look* at that in two days.

A note of caution to those who know French! Don't confuse a Haitian Creole sentence such as *Mari a chante* (Mary will sing) with a French sentence such as *Marie a chanté* (Mary has sung).

The Conditional Tense (Tan Kondisyonèl)

The conditional tense (the "would" form in English) is expressed by *ta* plus the verb:

Si m te gen lajan, m ta manje.	If I had money, I *would* eat.
Mwen *ta fè sa* tou.	I *would do* that too.
M *ta* renmen *wè* ou denmen.	I *would like* to see you tomorrow.
Mwen *ta* pito bliye sa.	I *would* prefer to forget that.
Si *m te* la, *m ta* pale ak li.	If I *were* there, I *would* talk with him/her.

We tend to mostly use the present tense of the conditional.

Commands (Enperatif)

Commands are similar to English in that the pronoun *ou* ("you") or *nou* ("you" plural) is left out. Commands in Haitian Creole are different from English in that they are usually followed, as a form of politeness, either by *wi* (for a strong request) or by *non* (for a less decided request). Much depends, naturally, upon the tone of voice used as well as the context.

Manje, wi!	Eat!
Soti, wi!	Leave!
Chita, non!	Won't you sit down!

Antre, non!	Won't you come in!
Ale Okap denmen!	Go to Cap-Haitian tomorrow!

The first person plural command form ("Let's . . .") is expressed by *An nou*, or by its shortened form Ann:

An nou **wè sa, wi!**	*Let's* see that!
Ann **ale pale ak yo jodi a!**	*Let's* go talk with them today!
Ann **etidye leson nou, non!**	*Let's* study our (your plural) lesson!

A **negative command** is expressed by *pa* before the verb, usually followed by a strong *non* (but never by a *wi*):

Pa **pale konsa, non!**	*Don't* talk like that!
Pa **ale nan mache jodi a!**	*Don't* go to the market today!
Annou pa **di l bonjou, non!**	*Let's* not say good day to him!
Ann pa **manje isit, non!**	*Let's* not eat here!

Helping Verbs

Helping verbs are used immediately preceding another verb and serve to modify the meaning of the second verb. Among the most common is *Fèk* = to have just (done something):

M *fèk* **wè li.**	I have *just* seen her.
Li *fèk* **fè sa.**	He's *just* done that.
Li *fèk* **fèt.**	He's *just* been born.

Another common helping verb is *Sot* = to have just (done something). This is the equivalent of the French *sortir*:

Se moun ki *sot* rive lavil.	He's someone who *has just* come into town.
Yo *sot* soti.	They've *just* gone out.
Lalin *sot* kache tèt li dèyè yon nyaj.	The moon's *just* hidden itself behind a cloud.

Mèt means may (to have permission to do something):

Ou *mèt* manje zoranj la.	You *may*/are permitted to eat the orange.
Telefòn lan lib kounye a; ou *mèt* rele zanmi ou a.	The phone's free now; you *may* call your friend.

Konn means to be in the habit of (doing something), to often (do something); to know how to (do something)

Li te *konn* travay rèd.	He *was in the habit* of working hard.
	He *used to* work hard.
Yo *konn* al lekòl le maten.	They *go* to school every morning.
Mwen *konn* naje.	I *know how* to swim.
Li *konn* pale panyòl.	He *knows how* to speak Spanish.
	He *often* speaks Spanish.

Fin means to finish (doing something):

Mari *fin* ede manman li.	Mary *finishes* helping her mother.
Lè yo te *fin* manje, yo te soti wè zanmi	When they *finished* eating, they went out to see some friends.
Lè l *fin* rive Jeremi, li te fatige anpil.	When he *finally* got to Jeremie, he was very tired.

Pral means to be going to (do something); to be going to:

M *pral* rele frè m.	I'm *going to* call my brother.
Eskize m! M *pral* fè yon ti soti.	Excuse me! I'm *going* out for a little while.
Zanmi m *pral* vini ede m pote kèk zouti.	My friend *is going to* come help me carry some tools.
M *pral* lapòs.	I'm *going to* the post office.

The Irregular Verb Bay (*Vèb Iregilye a* Bay)

Bay (to give) is Haitian Creole's one and only "irregular" verb (*mèsi, Bondye!*)—and it has only three forms. Bay changes form only when followed directly by one of the five pronouns.

Bay becomes *Ba* when followed directly by the pronouns *ou, li (l)*, or *yo*:

M ap *ba* ou li denmen.	I'll *give* it to you tomorrow.
M *ba* l di goud.	I *give* him ten gourdes.
M te *ba* yo yon ti bokal konfiti.	I *gave* them a little jar of jam.

Bay becomes *ban* when followed directly by the pronouns *mwen* (m') or *nou* (n'):

Ban mwen ti liv ble an souple.	*Give* me the little blue book, please.
Ban n van, wi!	*Give* us some space!
Apantè a pa te *ban* nou anyen, non!	The surveyor certainly didn't *give* us anything!

Bay stays *bay* when not followed directly by a pronoun. In other words, always use the form bay, except when followed immediately by a pronoun.

M te *bay moun* sa yo anpil kòb deja.	I've already *given* those people a lot of money.
Y ap *bay* Nana yon bèl ti bisiklèt wouj.	They're *giving* Nana a beautiful little red bicycle.
Nou *bay* Jòj yon gwo pwason.	We *give* George a big fish.

Bay can also be used as a preposition meaning "for," "to":

Li pote yon ti vè wonm *ban* mwen.	He brought a little glass of rum *for* me.
Matant mwen te konn li kèk paj Labib *ban* nou.	My aunt used to read several pages from the Bible *to* us.

Adjectives

Short, commonly used adjectives come before the noun they modify. The most important ones are used below:

M renmen ti **kay la.**	I like the *little* house.
Gwo **nèg la ap chita.**	The *fat* man is sitting down.
Li te jwenn li nan gran *wout* **la.**	He found it on the *main* road.
Se *bon* **moun ou ye.**	You're a *good* person.
Sa a se yon *move* **liv.**	That's a *bad* book.
Jenn **moun pa jenn bèt.**	A *young* person is not (permitted to act like) a *young* animal.
Li te achte yon *nouvo* **sentiwon.**	He bought a *new* belt.
Granmoun **fanm lan t ap manje.**	The *old* woman was eating.
Men yon *bèl* **fanm.**	Here's a *beautiful* woman.
M' gen yon *sèl* **bagay pou m di.**	I have only one *single* thing I have to say.
Se yon *vrè* **pwoblèm.**	It's a *real* problem.
Pa te gen yon *lòt* **bagay pou m fè.**	There was nothing *else* for me to do.
Kèk **zanmi te vin lakay li.**	*Several* friends came to his home.

The form *ti* ("small," "little") can only be used before the noun; to express "small," "little" as a predicate adjective, the form *piti* must be used:

Ti **kay la te bèl.**	The *little* house was nice-looking.
Kay la te *piti.*	The house was *small.*

Move means "bad, old, faulty, mean" when preceding the noun, but "angry" when used as a predicate adjective:

Move bourik la pa vle fè anyen.	The *no-good* donkey doesn't want to do anything.
Chèf la te *move* anpil.	The boss was very *angry*.

Pwòp is placed *before* the noun to mean "own" and *after* the noun to mean "clean":

Li te voye *pwòp* frè l wè yo.	He sent his *own* brother to see them.
Yon machin *pwòp* toujou pi bèl.	A *clean* car is always prettier.

Mechan ("bad, wicked, evil") takes on a figurative meaning for stress or exaggeration when *preceding* the noun:

Li te fè yon mechan **lapli.**	There was an *awful* rain.
Li te gen yon *mechan* lafyèv.	He had a *horrible* fever.
Ti gason *mechan* an te pouse l tonbe nan larivyè a.	The *bad/mean* little boy pushed him into the river.
Yo gen kèk gwo chen mechan.	They have several big *mean* dogs.

Other adjectives follow the noun:

Nèg *avèg* la rive lakay li.	The *blind* man arrives home.
Liv *ble* a sou tab la.	The *blue* book is on the table.
Kivèt *cho* a te tonbe atè.	The *hot* wash-basin fell on the ground.
Ban m chemiz *chire* sa a.	Give me that *torn* shirt.

Li gen tèt *di*, papa!	Man, he's *hard* headed!
Sak *vid* pa kanpe.	An *empty* bag doesn't stand up. (No work gets done on an *empty* stomach.)

Note especially the two following adjectives which are contrary to French usage:

Yon ti madmwazèl *janti* te prezante fim lan.	A *nice* young lady presented the film.
Li te rakonte nou yon istwa *long*.	He told us a *long* story.

Asking Questions

Unlike English or other languages, you do not need to use multiple ways of phrasing a question in Creole—it is fairly easy. The question does not require additional words other than what is necessary to ask a question.

Yes-No Questions

As in many languages, one of the most common ways of asking a question to be answered by "yes" (*wi*) or "no" (*non*) is simply by raising the pitch of the voice at the end:

Ou bouke.	You're tired.
Ou bouke?	You're tired?
Ou prale kounye a.	You're leaving now.
Ou prale kounye a?	You're leaving now?

For a greater clarity or emphasis *èske* can begin the question:

Ou bouke?   Are you tired?

   Or

Èske ou bouke?   Are you tired?
Ou prale kounye a?   Are you leaving now?

   Or

Èske ou prale kounye a?   Are you leaving now?

Information Questions

When more than just a yes-no answer is expected, a special word (or words) is placed normally at the beginning of the question:

Asking What with *Kisa* and *Sa* To ask "what" you can use the words *kisa* or *sa*. *Kisa* and *sa* are used interchangeably. *Sa* in the context of a question is a short form of *kisa*.

Kisa **ou wè kounye a?**   *What* do you see now?

   Or

Sa **ou wè kounye a?**   *What* do you see now?
Kisa **li vle fè?**   *What* does he/she/it want to do?

   Or

Sa **li vle fè?**   *What* does he/she/it want to do?

Asking How with *Kijan* and *Kouman* To ask how we use the words *kijan* or *kouman*. Neither *kijan* nor *kouman* has a shortened form.

Kijan ou ye?	*How* are you?

Or

Kouman ou ye?	*How* are you?
Kijan yo ka fè sa?	*How* can they do that?

Or

Kouman yo ka fè sa?	*How* can they do that?

Asking When with *Kilè* To ask when we use the word *kilè*. "Kilè" as a question word lacks a shortened version.

Kilè li vini?	*When* does he/she/it come?
Kilè nou ka manje?	*When* can we/you (plural) eat?

Asking Where with *Ki Kote* and *Kibò* *Ki kote* and *kibò* refer to where. They may be used interchangeably. *Ki kote* may be shortened to *kote*, but *kibò* is not shortened as a question word.

Ki kote ou rete?	*Where* do you live?

Or

Kote ou rete?	*Where* do you live?

Or

Kibò ou rete?	*Where* do you live?
Ki kote ou ale kounye a?	*Where* do you go now?

Or

Kote ou ale kounye a?	*Where* do you go now?

Or

Kibò ou ale kounye a?	*Where* do you go now?

Asking Who with *Kimoun* or *Kilès* To express who or whom, we use *kimoun* or *kilès*. Sometimes we become redundant and we use *kilès moun*. There are no shortened forms for these words.

Kimoun ki la?	*Who*'s there?
Ki moun ki te fè sa a?	*Who* did this?
Kilès k ap pale ak Odèt?	*Who* is speaking with Odette?
Kilès moun w ap pase nan betiz?	*Who* are you making fun of?

Asking How Much with *Konbyen* To express how much or how many, we use *Konbyen* for both. It does not matter whether it is singular or plural. *Konbyen* does not have a shortened form.

Konbyen lajan ou genyen?	*How much* money do you have?
Konbyen chen yo gen la?	*How many* dogs do they have there?

Asking Why with *Poukisa* Sometimes one hears *Pouki*? to ask why But *Poukisa* is used more frequently.

Poukisa ou pa vini avè m?	*Why* don't you come with me?
Poukisa ou di sa?	*Why* do you say that?

Asking Which with *Ki* or *Kilès* *Ki* or *kilès* is used in connection with a noun to express "which." *Ki* is used more often than kilès.

Ki vè ou pito?	*Which* glass do you prefer?
Nan *ki* liv ou te li sa a?	In *which* book did you read that?
Kilès machin y ap kondi?	*Which* car are they driving?

Note: Inversion of subject and verb like we found in English and French are never used in Haitian Creole.

Questions beginning with *ki* must be followed by a *ki*, when *ki* is used as a subject:

Ki moun ki te rele ou?	*Who* called you?
Kisa ki enterese ou?	*What* interests you?
Kilè ki ta bon pou ou?	*What time* would be good for you?
Ki kote ki te sal?	*Which* place was dirty?
Kibò ki te pwòp?	*Which* place was clean?

Contractions

Contractions and combinations of words are just as frequent in Haitian Creole as in English. Some of the main categories are:

I. Pronouns

Mwen = m.

M pa te wè l.   *I* didn't see him.

Nou = n

M kwè yo kab ede *n.*   I think they can help *us.*
                                     (or *you* pl.)

2. The Verb Modifier Ap

You consider *ap* as the "-ing" part of the verb. At least it is the one that tell us that we are facing a verb in English that needs an "-ing" ending. However, the part it represents is only where you have "is/are/am" or "was/were":

Mwen + ap = m ap.

M *ap* fè ou peye sa chè.   *I'll* make you pay dearly for that.

Li + ap = l ap.

L *ap* fè yo bati yon kay.   *He's* having them build a house.

Nou + ap = n ap.

N *ap* pati demen.   *We're* leaving tomorrow.

Yo + ap = y ap.

Si ou fè sa, *y ap* arete ou.   If you do that, *they'll* arrest you.

Ki + ap = k ap.

Men nèg la *k ap* ede m nan.   Here's the man *who's* helping
                                                                          me.

Pa + ap = p ap.

Li *p ap* travay ankò.   He/she *is* no longer working.

Te + ap = t ap.

Li *t ap* tape lèt la.   He/she *was* typing the letter.

3. The Future Indicator A

Mwen + a = m a.

M *a* wè ou pita, papa!   *I'll* see you later, man!

Li + a = l a.

L *a* ba ou li demen.   *She/He'll* give it to you
                                                                           tomorrow.

Nou + a = n a.

N *a* wè.   *We will* see.

Yo + a = y a.

Y *a* tounen nan de mwa.   *They'll* return in two months.

4. Pa t *and* Sa K

Abbreviation of *pa + te*: *pa + te = pa t* (did not).

M *pa t* jwenn li.	I *didn't* find it.
Li *pa t* bwè dlo a	He *did not* drink the water

Abbreviation of *kisa ki*: *Sa + ki = sa k* (what).

Men *sa k* rive.	Here's *what* (that, which) happened.

5. *Common Verbs*

Ale = al.

Tout moun desann lavil *al* vote.	Everyone goes down to town *to (go)* vote.

Fini = fin.

Lè yo *fin* lave tout rad yo, yo te vle dòmi.	When they *finished* washing all the clothes, they wanted to sleep.
M pa *gen* kòb menm!	I don't *have* any money at all.

Mete = met.

Yo te *met* tout bagay ladann.	They *put* everything in it.

Prale = pral.

Se madanm li ki *pral* sèvi l.	It's his wife who *is going* to serve him.

Vini = vin.

Fi sa a ap *vin* wè yo.	That lady is *coming* to see them.
Se pou sa tout moun *te vin* tris anpil.	That's why everyone *became* very sad.

This, That, These, and Those

"This" and "that" when used as an adjective are both expressed by *sa a*. The plural ("these," "those") is expressed by *sa yo*. The forms *sila a* ("that") and *sila yo* ("those") are used less often

Liv *sa a* itil anpil.	*This/that* book is very useful.
Ban m vè *sa a*, souple.	Give me *this/that* glass, please.
Ak moun *sa yo*, ou pa janm konnen.	With *these/those* people, you never know.
Nèg sa a fèk mande zaboka *sa yo*.	This/that man has just asked for *these/those* avocadoes.

When used as a pronoun both are normally expressed by *sa*; for special emphasis *Sa a* is used:

Kounye a m konprann *sa*.	Now I understand *this/that*.
Ak *sa*, ou kap fè anpil kòb.	With *this/that*, you can make a lot of money.
Papa! Èske ou te wè *sa a*?	Man! Did you see *this/that*?

Possession

Possession is expressed in three different ways, but for the purpose of this book we will focus on the simple way. In Creole, we can show possession by placing the person or thing possessed in front of the possessor (just the opposite of English)

Kay David	David's house
Zanmi Jan	John's friend
Zòrèy bourik la	The donkey's ear (s)
Non Mari	Mary's name

Placement of Objects

In a language where prepositions are used less frequently than in English or French, it is important to remember that the indirect object comes before the direct object.

Li te ban *m* liv la.	He gave the book *to me*.
Yo montre *nou* yo.	They show them *to us*.
Yo montre *yo* nou.	They show us *to them*.
Sa te fè *yo* twa pitit.	That made three children *for them*.
Nou te di *yo* bonjou.	We said good morning *to them*.
Li te ba *li* nouvèl la.	She told the news *to him*.
Li te aprann *li* nouvèl la.	She told *him* the news.

Positioning of Parts of Speech

The position of certain classes of words can present problems. The main problem areas are:

Articles

The five forms of the definite article (*la*, *a*, *an*, *lan*, *yo*) come not only after the noun they modify, but they also come after any adjective (s) or noun clause modifying the noun. The form of the definite article depends upon the *ending* of the immediately *preceding* word:

Kay *la*	*The* house
Kay pay *la*	*The* straw-roofed house
Kay pay moun sa yo te bati *a*	*The* straw-roofed house those people built
Machin *lan*	*The* car
Machin ble *a*	*The* blue car
Machin mwen *an*	My (specific) car (lit.: the my car)
Machin li te prete Tijak *la*	*The* car he lent Jack

The indefinite article (*yon*) comes before the noun it modified, just as in English:

Yon asyèt	*A* plate/a dish
Yon bokit	*A* bucket
Yon mwa	*A* month
Yon legliz	*A* church

Verb Modifiers

Verb modifiers are always placed before the verb:

Li *pa* wè l.	He doesn't see it.
Yo *te* ale lavil.	They *went* to town
Ou *ap* chante.	You are sing*ing*.
Mwen *ta* vle soti.	I *would* like to go out.
Jòj *a* fè sa demen.	George *will* do that tomorrow.
Te gen anpil pwoblèm.	There *were* a lot of problems.
Pral gen anpil pwoblèm.	There *will* be a lot of problems.

Two exceptions are *se te* and *se ta*.

Se te yon bon prezidan.	He *was* a good president.
Se ta malchans si li pa vini.	It *would* be unfortunate/ bad luck if he didn't come.

Possessive Pronouns (Pwonon Posesif)

Possessive pronouns are always placed after the noun:

Kay *mwen*	*My* house
Kabann *yo*	*Their* bed
Manman *m*	*My* mother
Machin *ou*	*Your* car

Note: the plural indicator *yo* comes *after* the possessive pronoun:

Kay mwen *yo*	*My* houses
Machin ou *yo*	*Your* cars

But *yo* (possessive pronoun) and *yo* (plural indicator) are never used together; thus, *machin yo a* can mean either "*their* car" or "*the* cars."

Anpil

Anpil is placed before a noun and after an adjective or verb:

Te gen *anpil moun* nan mache a.	There were *a lot of people* in the market.
***Anpil fwa* li pat vle vini.**	*Many times* he didn't want to come.
M te wè *anpil zannimo* sou wout la.	I saw *many animals* on the road.
Mwen *bouke* anpil jodi a.	I'm very *tired* today.
Yo te *kontan* wè l [*anpil*].	They were *very happy* to see her.
Se te yon kay ki te *gwo anpil*.	It was a house which was *very large*.
Pastè a te pale *anpil*.	The (Protestant) minister talked *a lot*.
Se yon moun k ap *travay anpil*.	He's a person who's *working a lot*.
Moun ki manje *anpil*, anpil fwa ou a wè yo gwo *anpil*.	People who eat *a lot*, *often* you will see they are *very* fat.

Appendix **B**

Verb Table

Sample Verbs

English Verb	Creole Present	Creole Past	Creole Future	Creole Conditional	Creole Present Progressive	Creole Past Progressive
Accompany	Ale ak	Te ale ak	A ale ak	Ta ale ak	Ap ale ak	T ap ale ak
Alleviate	Amelyore	Te amelyore	A amelyore	Ta amelyore	Ap amelyore	T ap amelyore
Avoid	Evite	Te evite	A evite	Ta evite	Ap evite	T ap evite
Awaken	Leve	Te leve	A leve	Ta leve	Ap leve	T ap leve
Bathe	Benyen	Te benyen	A benyen	Ta benyen	Ap benyen	T ap benyen
Begin	Kòmanse	Te kòmanse	A kòmanse	Ta kòmanse	Ap kòmanse	T ap kòmanse
Bite	Mòde	Te mòde	A mòde	Ta mòde	Ap mòde	T ap mòde
Bleed	Senyen	Te senyen	A senyen	Ta senyen	Ap senyen	T ap senyen
Blink	Bat je	Te bat je	A bat je	Ta bat je	Ap bat je	T ap bat je
Breastfeed	Bay tete	Te bay tete	A bay tete	Ta bay tete	Ap bay tete	T ap bay tete
Breathe	Respire	Te respire	A respire	Ta respire	Ap respire	T ap respire
Burp	Gobye	Te gobye	A gobye	Ta gobye	Ap gobye	T ap gobye
Call	Rele	Te rele	A rele	Ta rele	Ap rele	T ap rele
Defecate	Poupou	Te Poupou	A Poupou	Ta Poupou	Ap Poupou	T ap Poupou
Diet	Fè rejim	Te fè rejim	A fè rejim	Ta fè rejim	Ap fè rejim	T ap fè rejim

Disappear	Disparèt	Te disparèt	A disparèt	Ta disparèt	Ap disparèt	T ap disparèt
Dissolve	Delye	Te delye	A delye	Ta delye	Ap delye	T ap delye
Distinguish	Distenge	Te distenge	A distenge	Ta distenge	Ap distenge	T ap distenge
Draw	Trase	Te trase	A trase	Ta trase	Ap trase	T ap trase
Dress	Abiye	Te abiye	A abiye	Ta abiye	Ap abiye	T ap abiye
Drink	Bwè	Te bwè	A bwè	Ta bwè	Ap bwè	T ap bwè
(Get) drunk	Sou (be)	Te sou	A sou	Ta sou	Ap sou	T ap sou
Eat	Manje	Te manje	A manje	Ta manje	Ap manje	T ap manje
Ejaculate	Voye	Te voye	A voye	Ta voye	Ap voye	T ap voye
Examine	Egzaminen	Te egzaminen	A egzaminen	Ta egzaminen	Ap egzaminen	T ap egzaminen
Exercise	Fè egzèsis	Te fè egzèsis	A fè egzèsis	Ta fè egzèsis	Ap fè egzèsis	T ap fè egzèsis
Exhale	Lage souf	Te lage souf	A lage souf	Ta lage souf	Ap lage souf	T ap lage souf
Faint	Endispoze	Te endispoze	A endispoze	Ta endispoze	Ap endispoze	T ap endispoze
Fall down	Tonbe	Te tonbe	A tonbe	Ta tonbe	Ap tonbe	T ap tonbe
Feel, smell	Santi	Te santi	A santi	Ta santi	Ap santi	T ap santi
Fire (work)	Revoke	Te revoke	A revoke	Ta revoke	Ap revoke	T ap revoke
Focus	Fikse	Te fikse	A fikse	Ta fikse	Ap fikse	T ap fikse
Follow	Suiv	Te suiv	A suiv	Ta suiv	Ap suiv	T ap suiv

continued

Sample Verbs continued

English Verb	Creole Present	Creole Past	Creole Future	Creole Conditional	Creole Present Progressive	Creole Past Progressive
Fracture	fele	Te fele	A fele	Ta fele	Ap fele	T ap fele
Gargle	Gagari	Te gagari	A gagari	Ta gagari	Ap gagari	T ap gagari
Get up	Leve	Te leve	A leve	Ta leve	Ap leve	T ap leve
Give	Bay	Te bay	A bay	Ta bay	Ap bay	T ap bay
Go out	Soti	Te soti	A soti	Ta soti	Ap soti	T ap soti
Harm	Fè mal	Te fè mal	A fè mal	Ta fè mal	Ap fè mal	T ap fè mal
Hear	Tande	Te tande	A tande	Ta tande	Ap tande	T ap tande
Help	Ede	Te ede	A ede	Ta ede	Ap ede	T ap ede
Hit	Frape	Te frape	A frape	Ta frape	Ap frape	T ap frape
Hurt	Fè mal	Te fè mal	A fè mal	Ta fè mal	Ap fè mal	T ap fè mal
Inflate	Gonfle	Te gonfle	A gonfle	Ta gonfle	Ap gonfle	T ap gonfle
Inhale	Respire	Te respire	A respire	Ta respire	Ap respire	T ap respire
Inject	Bay piki	Te bay piki	A bay piki	Ta bay piki	Ap bay piki	T ap bay piki
Inspire	Enspire	Te enspire	A enspire	Ta enspire	Ap enspire	T ap enspire
Itch	Grate	Te grate	A grate	Ta grate	Ap grate	T ap grate

Keep	Kenbe	Te kenbe	A kenbe	Ta kenbe	Ap kenbe	T ap kenbe
Laugh	Ri	Te ri	A ri	Ta ri	Ap ri	T ap ri
Lean	Panche	Te panche	A panche	Ta panche	Ap panche	T ap panche
Learn	Aprann	Te aprann	A aprann	Ta aprann	Ap aprann	T ap aprann
Lie down	Kouche	Te kouche	A kouche	Ta kouche	Ap kouche	T ap kouche
Lift	Leve	Te leve	A leve	Ta leve	Ap leve	T ap leve
Look at	Gade	Te gade	A gade	Ta gade	Ap gade	T ap gade
Lose	Pèdi	Te pèdi	A pèdi	Ta pèdi	Ap pèdi	T ap pèdi
Make decisions	Deside	Te deside	A deside	Ta deside	Ap deside	T ap deside
Make love	Fè lanmou	Te fè lanmou	A fè lanmou	Ta fè lanmou	Ap fè lanmou	T ap fè lanmou
Marry	Marye	Te marye	A marye	Ta marye	Ap marye	T ap marye
Masturbate	Bat laponyèt	Te bat laponyèt	A bat laponyèt	Ta bat laponyèt	Ap bat laponyèt	T ap bat laponyèt
Menstruate	Gen règ	Te gen règ	A gen règ	Ta gen règ	Ap gen règ	T ap gen règ
Mix	Melanje	Te melanje	A melanje	Ta melanje	Ap melanje	T ap melanje
Move	Deplase	Te deplase	A deplase	Ta deplase	Ap deplase	T ap deplase
Be nauseated	Gen kè plen	Te gen kè plen	A gen kè plen	Ta gen kè plen	Ap gen kè plen	T ap gen kè plen
Open	Ouvri	Te ouvri	A ouvri	Ta ouvri	Ap ouvri	T ap ouvri
Operate	Opere	Te opere	A opere	Ta opere	Ap opere	T ap opere

continued

Sample Verbs continued

English Verb	Creole Present	Creole Past	Creole Future	Creole Conditional	Creole Present Progressive	Creole Past Progressive
Pay	Peye	Te peye	A peye	Ta peye	Ap peye	T ap peye
Perspire	Swe	Te swe	A swe	Ta swe	Ap swe	T ap swe
To be pregnant	Gwòs/ansent	Te gwòs/ansenr	A gwòs/ansent	Ta gwòs/ansent	Ap gwòs/ansent	T ap gwòs/ansent
Push	Pouse	Te pouse	A pouse	Ta pouse	Ap pouse	T ap pouse
Put	Mete	Te mete	A mete	Ta mete	Ap mete	T ap mete
Raise	Leve	Te leve	A leve	Ta leve	Ap leve	T ap leve
Read	Li	Te li	A li	Ta li	Ap li	T ap li
Reassure	Rasire	Te rasire	A rasire	Ta rasire	Ap rasire	T ap rasire
Recover	Refè	Te refè	A refè	Ta refè	Ap refè	T ap refè
Relax	Kalme (li)	Te kalme	A kalme	Ta kalme	Ap kalme	T ap kalme
Remember	Sonje	Te sonje	A sonje	Ta sonje	Ap sonje	T ap sonje
Remove	Retire	Te retire	A retire	Ta retire	Ap retire	T ap retire
Repeat	Repete	Te repete	A repete	Ta repete	Ap repete	T ap repete
Rest	Repoze	Te repoze	A repoze	Ta repoze	Ap repoze	T ap repoze
Retain	Kenbe	Te kenbe	A kenbe	Ta kenbe	Ap kenbe	T ap kenbe

Say	Di	Te di	A di	Ta di	Ap di	T ap di
Scratch	Grate	Te grate	A grate	Ta grate	Ap grate	T ap grate
See	Wè	Te wè	A wè	Ta wè	Ap wè	T ap wè
Shave	Fè bab	Te fè bab	A fè bab	Ta fè bab	Ap fè bab	T ap fè bab
Shout	Rele	Te rele	A rele	Ta rele	Ap rele	T ap rele
Show	Montre	Te montre	A montre	Ta montre	Ap montre	T ap montre
Sign	Siyen	Te siyen	A siyen	Ta siyen	Ap siyen	T ap siyen
Sit down	Chita	Te chita	A chita	Ta chita	Ap chita	T ap chita
Sit up	Leve chita*	Te leve chita	A leve chita	Ta leve chita	Ap leve chita	T ap leve chita
Sleep	Dòmi	Te dòmi	A dòmi	Ta dòmi	Ap dòmi	T ap dòmi
Smell, feel	Santi	Te santi	A santi	Ta santi	Ap santi	T ap santi
Smile	Souri	Te souri	A souri	Ta souri	Ap souri	T ap souri
Smoke	Fimen	Te fimen	A fimen	Ta fimen	Ap fimen	T ap fimen
Sneeze	Estènen	Te estènen	A estènen	Ta estènen	Ap estènen	T ap estènen
Speak	Pale	Te pale	A pale	Ta pale	Ap pale	T ap pale
Spell	Eple	Te eple	A eple	Ta eple	Ap eple	T ap eple
Spend (money)	Depanse	Te depanse	A depanse	Ta depanse	Ap depanse	T ap depanse

*This verb is used when it is obvious that the person is lying down or not sitting straight.

continued

Sample Verbs continued

English Verb	Creole Present	Creole Past	Creole Future	Creole Conditional	Creole Present Progressive	Creole Past Progressive
Spend (time)	Pase	Te pase	A pase	Ta pase	Ap pase	T ap pase
Squeeze	Peze	Te peze	A peze	Ta peze	Ap peze	T ap peze
Stand	Kanpe	Te kanpe	A kanpe	Ta kanpe	Ap kanpe	T ap kanpe
Stick out	File deyò	Te file deyò	A file deyò	Ta file deyò	Ap file deyò	T ap file deyò
Straighten out	Drese	Te drese	A drese	Ta drese	Ap drese	T ap drese
Subtract	Retire	Te retire	A retire	Ta retire	Ap retire	T ap retire
Swallow	Vale	Te vale	A vale	Ta vale	Ap vale	T ap vale
Sweat	Swe	Te swe	A swe	Ta swe	Ap swe	T ap swe
Swell	Anfle	Te anfle	A anfle	Ta anfle	Ap anfle	T ap anfle
Take pulse	Pran pou(l)	Te pran pou(l)	A pran pou(l)	Ta pran pou(l)	Ap pran pou(l)	T ap pran pou(l)
Talk	Pale	Te pale	A pale	Ta pale	Ap pale	T ap pale
Taste	Goute	Te goute	A goute	Ta goute	Ap goute	T ap goute
Tell	Di	Te di	A di	Ta di	Ap di	T ap di
Threaten	Mennase	Te mennase	A mennase	Ta mennase	Ap mennase	T ap mennase
(Be) tired	Fatige	Te fatige	A fatige	Ta fatige	Ap fatige	T ap fatige

Touch	Touche	Te touche	A touche	Ta touche	Ap touche	T ap touche
Turn over	Tounen (kò)	Te Tounen (kò)	A Tounen (kò)	Ta Tounen (kò)	Ap Tounen (kò)	T ap Tounen (kò)
Understand	Konprann	Te konprann	A konprann	Ta konprann	Ap konprann	T ap konprann
Undress	Dezabiye	Te dezabiye	A dezabiye	Ta dezabiye	Ap dezabiye	T ap dezabiye
(Be)upset	Fache	Te fache	A fache	Ta fache	Ap fache	T ap fache
Urinate	Pipi	Te pipi	A pipi	Ta pipi	Ap pipi	T ap pipi
Vomit	Vonmi	Te vonmi	A vonmi	Ta vonmi	Ap vonmi	T ap vonmi
Wait	Tann	Te tann	A tann	Ta tann	Ap tann	T ap tann
Walk	Mache	Te mache	A mache	Ta mache	Ap mache	T ap mache
Wash	Lave	Te lave	A lave	Ta lave	Ap lave	T ap lave
Weigh	Peze	Te peze	A peze	Ta peze	Ap peze	T ap peze
(Get) wet	Mouye	Te mouye	A mouye	Ta mouye	Ap mouye	T ap mouye
Whistle	Sifle	Te sifle	A sifle	Ta sifle	Ap sifle	T ap sifle
Work	Travay	Te travay	A travay	Ta travay	Ap travay	T ap travay
Worry	Fatige (tèt)	Te fatige (tèt)	A fatige (tèt)	Ta fatige (tèt)	Ap fatige (tèt)	T ap fatige (tèt)
Worsen	Vin pi mal	Te vin pi mal	A vin pi mal	Ta vin pi mal	Ap vin pi mal	T ap vin pi mal
Write	Ekri	Te ekri	A ekri	Ta ekri	Ap ekri	T ap ekri

English to Creole Glossary

English	Creole
A	
above	anwo
accident	aksidan
address	adrès
administrator	administratè
affect	afekte
afraid	pè
after	aprè [apre]
after shocks	sekous aprè tranbleman
aftermath	konsekans/ annaprè
afternoon	aprèmidi
age	laj
agency	ajans
agronomist	agronòm
air	lè, è

English	Creole
air conditioner	è kondisyone
airline	konpayi avyon
airmail	kourye avyon
airmail envelope	anvlòp avyon
airplane	avyon
airport	ayewopò
alive	vivan
all	tout
allergic	alèji
also/too	tou/ositou
although	kwake
A.M.	maten
ambulance	anbilans
America	Lamerik/ Etazini
American	Ameriken/ Meriken

English	Creole
American dollar	dola Ameriken/ dola vèt
amount	kantite
amputate	koupe
ancient	ansyen
and	ak/epi
angry	fache/move
another	yon lòt
antibiotic	antibyotik
apartment	kay/apatman
appeal	apèl
appetizers	goute
appointment	randevou
April	avril
architect	achitèk
arm	bra
army	lame
arrange	ranje/òganize
arrival	rive/ateri
art	a/atizana
artist	atis
ask	mande
assistance	asistans
assistant	asistan
associate	asosye
at	a
ATM	Machin pou moun al retire lajan nan bank

English	Creole
attention	atansyon
August	out/dawou
aunt	matant/tant
automatic	otomatik
autumn	otòn
available	disponib
avenue	avni
avocado	zaboka

B

English	Creole
back	do
back (*v.*)	retounen
backache	maldo
bad	mal
bag	sak/sachè/valiz/ malèt
baker	boulanje
bakery	boulanjri/ boulanje
banana	fig
bank	bank
Baptist	batis
bar	ba
barbed wire	fildefè
bargaining	machande/ fè pri
basic	preliminè/ fondamantal
basketball	baskètbòl
bathroom	twalèt

English	Creole
battery	batri/pil
beans	pwa
beans and rice	pwa ak diri
beard	bab
beautiful	bèl
because	paske
bed	kabann
bedroom	chanm
beer	byè
before	anvan
begin	koumanse
behind	dèyè
beside	akote/kote/ bò kote
better	pi bon/miyò
between	ant/nan mitan/ omilye
big	gwo
bike	bekàn/bisiklèt
bill	bòdwo/fakti/ dèt
biology	byoloji
birth control	planin/grenn
birthday	fèt/anivèsè
black	nwa
black market	mache nwa
blanket	lèn
blond	jòn/blon
blood	san
blue	ble

English	Creole
boat	bato/batiman
body	kò
boiled	bouyi
bone	zo
book	liv
bookstore	libreri
boots	bòt
border	fwontyè
border crossing	janbe fwontyè
borderland	teritwa ki sou fwontyè
boss	patwon/chèf
bottled water	dlo boutèy
boundary	fwontyè/limit/ lizyè
bowl	bòl
box	bwat
boyfriend	mennaj
brakes	fren
Brazilian	brezilyen
bread	pen
break	kase/kraze/ brize
breakfast	dejennen/manje maten
brick	brik
bridge	pon
bring	pote/mennen
broadcast	emisyon (*n*.)/ fè emisyon

English	Creole	English	Creole
broken	kase/kraze	camp	kan
brother	frè	Canada	Kanada
brown	mawon	Canadian	Kanadyen
brush	bwòs	Canadian dollar	dola Kanadyen
bucket	bokit	car	machin/oto
build (v)	bati/konstwi	car rental	lwe machin
building	batiman	careful	atansyon
building code	regleman pou bati kay	Carnaval	Kanaval
		cash	kach
bulb	anpoul	cashier	kesye (*m.*)/ kesyè (*f.*)
bulldozer	bouldozè		
bureaucracy	biwokrasi	casino	kazino
burial	antèman	catastrophe	katastwòf
burn	boule	Catholic	Katolik
bury	antere	cement	siman
bus	bis/otobis	centimeter	santimèt
business	jesyon/biznis	cereal	sereyal
businessman	biznismann	change (*n.*)	chanjman
busy	okipe	change (*v.*)	chanje
but	men	cheap	bon mache/ pa chè
butcher shop	bouchri		
butter	bè	check	chèk
buy	achte	checkpoint	pòs kontwòl
by	pre/sou kote, bò/pa	cheese	fwomaj
		chemicals	chimik/pwodwi chimik

C

English	Creole	English	Creole
cable	fil/kab	chest	pwatrin/kòf lestomak
call	apèl/rele		
calm	kal	chicken	poul
camera	kamera	child/children	pitit/timoun
		Christmas	nwèl

English	Creole	English	Creole
church	legliz	confusion	konfizyon/dezòd
cinema	sinema		
cinnamon	kanèl	construction	konstriksyon
city	lavil/vil	construction site	chantye
civil	sivil	consultant	konsiltan
clean	netwaye	context	kontèks
clean	pwòp/lave	continent	kontinan
clinic	klinik	contract	kontra
clock	revèy/pandil	contribute	kontribye
close	fèmen	cook (n.)	kizinye
close (v.)	fèmen	cook (v.)	kwit
close/near	pre/pa lwen	cooperation	koperasyon
clothes	rad	copy	kopi/kopye
clothing	rad	corn	mayi
clove	jiwòf	corner	kwen/kafou
club	klib	corpses	kò/mò/kadav
coworker	kòlèg	corruption	magouy/pouriti
coffee	kafe	cost	pri/koute
cold	frèt	cough	tous/grip
collapse	tonbe/ekoule/kraze	country	peyi
		court	tribinal
color	koulè	cover	kouvèti/pwoteksyon
come	vini		
comfort	konfò	crack	fele/fisire/fann
community	kominotè	credit card	kat kredi
company	konpayi/sosyete	crowd	foul moun
computer	òdinatè/konpitè	crowd	foul
concerned	enkyete/angwase	crowded	gen anpil moun
concert	konsè	cruceiro (Brazilian)	krisero
concrete	beton		

English	Creole
cup	tas
customs	ladwann
cyber café	sibè kafe

D

English	Creole
damage	dega
dance	danse
danger	danje
dangerous	danjere
dark (color)	fonse
dark (night)	fè nwa
daughter	pitit fi
day	jou
death	lanmò
death toll	bilan lanmò
debris	fatra
December	desanm
decomposition	dekonpozisyon
delicious	bon/bon gou
demolish	efondre/detwi/demoli
demonstration	demonstrasyon
dentist	dantis
departure	pati/kite/ale
deploy	mete deyò
destroy	kraze/brize/detwi
destruction	destriksyon
devastate	devaste/sakaje/ravaje
dictionary	diksyonè

English	Creole
difficult	difisil
dig	fouye
dinner	soupe
dirt	tè/salte
dirty	sal
disorder	dezòd
dispatch	voye/ekspedye
dispensary	dispansè
displaced	deplase
divorced	divòse
dizzy	tèt vire
doctor	doktè
Doctors Without Borders	Doktè San Fwontyè
dog	chen
dollar	dola
Don't move!	Pa bouje!
Don't shoot!	Pa tire!
door	pòt
downtown	lavil/sant vil/anba lavil
dozen	douzenn
drawing	desen
dress	wòb
dress (*v.*)	abiye
drink (*n.*)	bwason
drink (*v.*)	bwè
drinking and driving	kondi machin sou
drive	kondi

English	Creole
driver	chofè/kondiktè
driver's license	lisans
drought	sechrès
dry	sèk/sèch/seche
dry cleaning	dray
dump	depo fatra
dump truck	kamyon fatra
dust	pousyè
DVD	dvd (Devede)

E

English	Creole
E-mail	Imèl/Mèl
ear	zòrèy
ear infection	enfeksyon nan zòrèy
earthquake	tranbleman/ tranblemanntè/ goudougoudou
east	ès/lès
Easter	Pak/Fèt Pak
eat	manje
economy	ekonomi
eggplant	berejèn
eggs	ze
electricity	elektrisite/ kouran
elevator	asansè
embassy	anbasad
emergency plan	egzèsis ijans
employee	anplwaye/moun k ap travay

English	Creole
employer	anplwayè/ patwon/ moun ki bay travay
engaged	angaje/okipe/ fiyanse
engineer	enjenyè
English	angle
enough	ase
entrance	antre
envelope	anvlòp
epicenter	episant
equal	egal
equipment	ekipman
euro	ero
evacuation	evakyasyon
examination	konsiltasyon/ egzamen
excellent	ekselan
Excuse me.	Eskize mwen.
exhibit	dokimantasyon/ prèv/ ekspozisyon
exit	sòti
expedition	ekspedisyon
expensive	chè
expire	ekspire/fini/ pase mòd/ gate
eye	je
eyedrops	gout pou je

English	Creole
F	
fabric	twal
face	fas/figi/devan/ gade anfas/ afwonte
fall (*v., n.*)	tonbe/otòn
family	lafanmi
fan	vantilatè
far	lwen/pa pre
farmer	kiltivatè
fast	vit
fat	gwo
father	papa
fax	faks/telekopi
fear	pè/laperèz
February	fevriye
feel	santi/touche/ manyen
feet	pye
female	fanm/fi
festival	festival
fever	lafyèv/fyèv
few	kèk
field director	direktè sou plas
fifth	senkyèm
fill	ranpli/plen
film	fim/sinema
financial	finansyè/ ekonomik
finger	dwèt

English	Creole
first	premye
first aid	premye sekou
fish	pwason
fishing	pèch/lapèch
flashlight	flash
flat tire	pàn kawotchou/ kawotchou plat
flight	vòl
flour	farin
food	manje
foot	pye
for	pou/paske/ poutèt/akòz
foreign aid	èd etranje
foreman	bòs/fòmann
forget	bliye
fork	fouchèt
form	fòm/dokiman
fourth	katryèm
fresh	fre
Friday	vandredi
friend	zanmi
from	apati de
from . . . to	de...a/soti... rive
front, in	devan
fruits	fri
full	plen
fund-raising	kolekte lajan
future	avni

English	Creole
G	
garbage	fatra
garbage dump	depo fatra
garbage truck	kamyon fatra
gas	gaz
gas station	ponp gazolin/ estasyon gazolin
gate	pòtay/baryè
gathering	rasanbleman
gender	sèks moun nan/ jan (maskilen/ feminen)
general	jeneral
generous	kè nan men
get	jwenn/resevwa/ gen/pran
gift	kado
ginger	jenjanm
girlfriend	mennaj
glass	vè
glasses	linèt
go away	pati/ale
Go!	Ale! Derape!
goat	kabrit
God	Bondye/ Granmèt/ Letènèl
God bless you.	Ke Bondye beni ou.
God willing	si Bondye vle

English	Creole
godfather	parenn
godmother	marenn
gold	lò
good	bon
Good morning.	Bonjou.
Good night.	Bonswa./ Bòn nwit.
Good-bye	M ale/orevwa
good(s)	machandiz/ danre
gram	gram
grandfather	granpapa/granpè
grandmother	grann/granmè
grave	tonm/fòs
great	gran/gwo
green	vèt
greetings	salitasyon
grey	gri
groceries	mache/ pwovizyon
group	gwoup
guest	envite/vizitè
guide	gid
gynecologist	jinekològ
H	
hair	cheve
haircut	fè tèt/koupe cheve
half	mwatye
half liter	mwatye lit

187

English	Creole
hall	koulwa
hammer	mato
hand	men
hanger	sèso
have	genyen/gen
he	li
head	tèt
headache	maltèt
health	sante/lasante
healthy	bòn sante/ ansante/gaya
hear	tande
heart	kè
heavy	lou
Hello	Alo/Bonjou/ Bonswa
help	ede
Help!	Anmwe!/Sekou!
helpful	itil
highway	wout nasyonal
history	istwa
holiday	fèt/konje/vakans
homeless	san kay
honor	onè/distenksyon
hospital	lopital
hospitality	ospitalite
hospitalize	entène (lopital)
hot	cho
hot pepper	piman bouk
hotel	otèl
hour	è/lè/èdtan

English	Creole
house	kay
How far?	Ki distans?
How long?	Depi kilè?
How many?	Konbyen?
How much?	Konbyen?
How?	Kijan?/ Kouman?/ Kòman?
humid	imid/mouye
hungry	grangou
hurricane	siklòn
Hurry!	Kouri!/Fè vit!/ Prese!
hurt	blese
husband	mari

I

I	mwen
ice cream	krèm
identification	idantifikasyon
if	si
illegal	ilegal
immediately	touswit/ imedyatman/ san pèdi tan
important	enpòtan
in front of	devan
inch	pous
inexpensive	bon mache
information	enfòmasyon
infrastructure	enfrastrikti

English	Creole
injured	blese
inside	andedan
inspection	enspeksyon
insurance	asirans
international	entènasyonal
Internet	entènèt
introduction	entwodiksyon/ prezantasyon
investigation	ankèt
invite	envite
island	zile

J

January	Janvye
jewelry	bijou
job	djòb/travay
jogging	kouri/djògin
journalism	jounalis/laprès
journalist	jounalis
journey	vwayaj/wout
judge	jij
juice	ji
July	Jiyè
jump drive	kle USB
June	jen

K

key	kle
kill	touye
killed	mouri
kilo	kilogram

English	Creole
kilogram	kilogram
kilometer	kilomèt
kitchen	kizin
knife	kouto
know	konnen

L

lab	laboratwa
lab test	egzamen laboratwa
ladder	echèl
lake	lak/lak dlo
land	tè/teren
landmark	pwen de repè
landscape	peyizaj
laptop	òdinatè/laptòp
large	laj/gwo
late	reta
later	pita
launch	koumanse
laundry	lave rad/lesiv
lawyer	avoka
leave	kite/ale/lese/pati
left	agoch
leg	janm
lemon	sitwon
lesson	leson
letter	lèt
lettuce	leti
library	bibliyotèk
license	patant/pèmi

English	Creole	English	Creole
lie (*v., n.*)	manti	map	kat jeografik
light	limyè	March	mas
like	renmen	market	mache
likeable	emab	married	marye
liter	lit	mask	mas
little	piti	mass graves	fòs komin/
living room	salon		chanyè
local	lokal/peyi/	matches	alimèt
	natif natal	math	matematik
long	long	May	me
look for	chache	maybe	petèt
looting	piyay/vòlè	meal	manje
lose	pèdi	measure	mezire
love	lanmou/	meat	vyann
	renmen	mechanic	mekanisyen
lunch	dine	media	medya (jounal,
			televizyon,
M			radyo)
machine	machin	medical	medikal
magazine	magazin	medicine	medsin
magnitude	fòs/pwisans	meeting	randevou/
mail	lèt		rankont/
mailbox	bwat lèt		reyinyon
mailman	faktè	menu	meni
male	gason	merchant	machann
man	nèg/gason/	meter	mèt
	nonm/	Mexican	meksiken
manager	direktè/manajè/	midnight	minwi
	responsab	mile	mil
many/a lot	anpil	milk	lèt

English	Creole	English	Creole
ministry	ministè	near	pre
minute	minit	neck	kou
missing	moun ki pèdi	need	bezwen
mission	misyon	neighbor	vwazinaj
mistake	erè/fòt	nephew	neve
mister (Mr.)	mesye	new	nouvo/jenn/ nèf
mobilize	mobilize		
moderate	modere	New Year	Premye Janvye/ Nouvo Ane
modern	modèn		
Monday	lendi	news	nouvèl/ enfòmasyon
money	lajan		
month	mwa	newspaper	jounal
moon	lalin	next	pwochèn/lòt
more	plis	nice	bon/janti/emab
morgues	mòg	niece	nyès
mother	manman	night	lannwit/nwit
mouth	bouch	no	non/okenn
Move!	Deplase!/ Bouje!	noise	bri
		Non-government organization (NGO)	Òganizasyon ki pa afilye ak gouvènman (ONG)
movie	fim/sinema		
Mr.	Mesye		
Mrs.	Madanm		
Ms.	Madmwazèl	non-stop	san rete/san poze
much	anpil		
museum	mize	noon	midi
music	mizik	north	nò
		not	pa/non
N		not far	pa lwen
nation	nasyon	November	novanm
national	nasyonal	now	kounye a

English	Creole	English	Creole
number	nonm/chif/ nimewo	original	orijinal
		ought	dwe/oblije
nurse	mis/enfimyè	over	anwo/anlè
		over there	lòt bò

O

English	Creole
object	objè/bagay/bi/ objektif
occupation	okipasyon
ocean	oseyan/gwo espas dlo lanmè
October	oktòb
odor	odè
office	biwo
officer	ofisye
official	ofisyèl
official visit	vizit ofisyèl
oil	lwil
OK	OK/oke
on	sou
on top of	sou
one way	sans inik/ki ale nan yon sèl direksyon
onions	zonyon
open	ouvri
operator	operatè
opinion	opinyon
or	ou byen
orange	zorany
order	lòd

P

English	Creole
package	pake
pain	doulè
painkiller	remèd doulè
pants	pantalon
Pardon me.	Eskize mwen.
park (a car)	pake/gare
parking lot	pakin/kote pou pake
party	fèt/pati
pass	pas
passport	paspò
pastor	pastè
patient	malad/pasyan
peace	lapè
peanuts	pistach
pen	plim
pencil	kreyon
people	moun
pepper	pwav
per day	pa jou
per hour	pa è
per month	pa mwa
per week	pa senmenn
percent	pousan
personal check	chèk pèsonèl

English	Creole
peso (Dominican)	peso
pharmacist	famasyen
pharmacy	famasi
phase	etap/faz
photo	foto
photographer	fotograf
phrase	fraz
physician	doktè
pick up	pran/ramase
picture	imaj/foto/pòtrè
piece	ti kal
pill	grenn (remèd)
pillow	zorye
pipe	tiyo
place	plas/espas/kote
plane	avyon
plantain	bannann
plastic	plastik
play (n.)	pyès teyat/jwèt
play (v.)	jwe/amize
please	tanpri/souple
pledge	angajman
plumber	plonbye
P.M.	aprèmidi
police	lapolis
police station	pòs polis
pork	kochon
post office	lapòs
postcard	kat postal
potatoes	pòmdetè

English	Creole
prefer	prefere
preference	preferans
pregnant	ansent/gwòs
prescription	preskripsyon
present	prezan
present (gift)	kado
price	pri
priest	pè
prioritize	plase an premye
prison	prizon
private	prive
problem	pwoblèm/ka
program	pwogram
project	pwojè
protection	pwoteksyon
Protestant	Pwotestan/ Levanjil
public	piblik
public services	sèvis piblik
pull out	retire/sòti/rale
pump	ponp
purple	mov
push	pouse
put	mete

Q

quarter	yon ka/eka
question	kesyon/ kesyone
quick	rapid

English	Creole
R	
radio	radyo/aparèy
radio station	pòs radyo
rain	lapli
rain gear	bagay pou lapli
read	li/fè lekti
rebuild	rebati/rekonstri
receipt	resi
recipe	resèt
reconstruction	rekonstriksyon
record (*n.*)	rapò
record (*v.*)	bay rapò/ anrejistre
red	wouj
Red Cross	Lakwa Wouj
refugee	refijye
relatives	fanmi/paran
relief	èd/soulajman
relief effort	efò pou ede/ pote sekou
religion	relijyon
remove	retire
rental car	machin lokasyon
renew	renouvle
repair	repare
reporter	jounalis
represent	reprezante
representative	reprezantatif
rescue	libere/sove

English	Creole
reservation	rezèvasyon
resources	resous/èd
responsibility	responsabilite
restaurant	restoran
restoration	repare/ranje
return	retounen
revolution	revolisyon
rice	diri
Richter scale	Echel Richtè
right	dwat
rioting	pwotestasyon/ revandikasyon
risk	risk
river	rivyè
road	wout
roasted	griye/woti/ babekyou
rock	wòch
room	chanm
room and board	pansyon
round-trip	ale retou
rubble	fatra/debri/ dekonm
rum	wonm
S	
safety	sekirite
salad	salad
salary	salè/tcho tcho
salt	sèl

English	Creole	English	Creole
sandals	sandal	shoes	soulye
Saturday	samdi	shop	magazen/
save (*v.*)	ekonomize		boutik/chòp/
savings	epay		atelye
say	di	short	kout
school	lekòl	shorts	chòt/bout
scissors	sizo		pantalon
scream	rele	shot (*n.*)	vaksen
screwdriver	tounvis	shot (*v.*)	tire
sea	lanmè	show	montre
seafood	fridemè	shower	douch
seaport	waf	shrimp	chèvrèt
search	chèche/chache/	sick	malad
	fouye	sickness	maladi
season	sezon	sidewalk	twotwa
seat	chita/chèz	sign	siy/pankat/jès
second	dezyèm	signature	siyati
security	sekirite	single	sèl/selibatè
security police	polis sekirite	sister	sè
see	wè	sit down	chita
send	voye	skinny	mèg/chèch
September	Septanm	skirt	jip
services	sèvis	sleep	dòmi
shampoo	chanpou	slow	lan/lantman/
she	li		dousman
shelter	kote pou dòmi/	Slow down!	Ralanti!
	kay pou dòmi	small	piti
shirt	chemiz	small change	ti lajan/ti
shoe shine	chany		monnen
shoemaker	kòdonye	smoke (*v.*)	fimen

English	Creole	English	Creole
smoke (*n.*)	lafimen	stay	rete
snapper	pwason woz	Stay away!/	Rete lwen!
sneakers	tenis	Keep your	
sneeze	estènen/estènye	distance!	
soap	savon		
soccer	foutbòl	steak	biftèk
socks	chosèt	steal	vòlè
soda	kola	stomach	vant
solar	solè	stone	galèt/wòch/pyè
soldier	sòlda	stop	estòp
solve	rezoud	Stop!	Kanpe!/Rete!
son	pitit gason	store (*v.*)	sere/anpile/
sore throat	gòj fèmal		konsève
sorry	padon/eskize	straight	dwat
	mwen	straight ahead	dwat devan ou
south	sid	street	lari
souvenirs	souvni	street food	aleken/manje
spaghetti	espageti		kwit
sparkling water	dlo kabonate	strike	grèv
speak	pale	student	elèv/etidyan
speed	vitès	study	etidye
spices	epis	suddenly	bridsoukou
spoon	kiyè	suffer	soufri/pase
spring	prentan		mizè
square (shape)	kare	sugar	sik
stamp(s)	tenm	summer	ete/lete
standard	estanda/kritè/	sun	solèy
	nòmal	Sunday	dimanch
start	koumanse	supermarket	makèt
statue	estati	supper	soupe
		surgeon	chirijyen

English	Creole
survive	moun ki chape/moun ki sove
sweater	chanday/sitè
swim	naje
swimming suit	kostim deben
symptoms	sentòm
syringe	sereng

T

English	Creole
table	tab
Take care.	Okipe./Pran swen.
tall	wo
tape	riban
tax	taks/enpo
taxi	taksi
tea	te
teacher/professor	profesè
technician	teknisyen
telephone	telefòn/telefone
telethon	teleton
television	televizyon
tell	di/pale/rakonte
teller/cashier	kesye
temperature	tanperati
temple	tanp
tent	tant
Thank you.	Mèsi.
theater	teyat

English	Creole
theft	vòl
there	la/la a
they	yo
thief	vòlè/vòlèz
thing	bagay
think (*v.*)	panse
third	twazyèm
thirsty	swaf
threat	menas
throat	gòj
Thursday	jedi
ticket	tikè/biyè
tie	kravat/kòl
time	fwa/lè/moman
tip	tip/poubwa
tire	kawoutchou
tired	fatige
to	a/nan
today	jodi a
together	ansanm
toilet	twalèt
toiletries	bagay pou fè twalèt/bagay pou pwòpte kò
tomatoes	tomat
tomorrow	demen
tongue	lang
tonight	aswè a
too much	twòp

English	Creole
tool	zouti
tooth/teeth	dan
toothache	maldan
toothbrush	bwòs dan
toothpaste	pat
tornado	tònad/toubiyon
touch	touche
tourist	touris
towel	sèvyèt
town	vil/lavil
toxic	toksik
tractor	traktè
traffic	sikilasyon/ anbouteyaj
trafficker	trafikan
translate	tradwi
translation	tradiksyon
trapped	kwense
trash	fatra
trauma	chòk/twoma
travel	vwayaje
traveler's check	chèk vwayaj
treatment	tretman
tremors	sekous
trip	vwayaj
truck	kamyon
truck drivers	chofè kamyon
trunk	kòf machin
T-shirt	mayo
tsunami	sounami
Tuesday	madi

English	Creole
U	
umbrella	parapli/onbrèl
uncle	monnonk/ tonton
under	anba
under/below	anba
understand	konprann
UNICEF	INISEF
United Nations	Nasyonzini
United States	Etazini
university	inivèsite
unrest	ajitasyon
until	jiska/jis/ annatandan/ jiskaske
up	anlè/anwo/soutèt
urgent	ijan
urine	pipi
U.S. Aid	èd Ameriken
V	
vegetables	legim
very much	anpil
victim	viktim
video	videyo
view	wè/gade/ egzamine
vinegar	vinèg
visa	viza
vitamin	vitamin
Vodou	Vodou

English	Creole	English	Creole
W		Wednesday	mèkredi
wait	tann	week	senmenn
waiter	sèvè	west	lwès
waiting	tann	white	blan
waiting room	sal datant	wife	madanm
waitress	madanm/	will	testaman
	madmwazèl	wind	van
walk	mache	window	fenèt
wall	mi	wine	diven
wallet	bous/pòtfèy	wishes	souwè
want	vle	woman	fi/fanm/
war	lagè		madanm
warehouse	depo	work	travay
warm	tyèd	worker	travayè
warning	avi/avètisman	wounded	blese
wash	lave	wrong	pa bon
watch	gade/siveye		
water	dlo	**XYZ**	
watermelon	melon	year	ane
we	nou	yellow	jòn
weak	fèb	yes	wi
weapon	zam	yogurt	yawou
weather	tan	you	ou

For Further Reading

Accilien, Adams, and Méléance. *Revolutionary Freedoms: A History of Survival, Strength & Imagination in Haiti.* Coconut Creek, FL: Caribbean Studies Press, 2006.

Arthur, Charles. *Haiti in Focus: A Guide to the People, Politics & Culture.* Brooklyn, NY: Interlink Publishing Group, 2001.

Arthur, Charles, and Michael J. Dash (editors). *Libète: A Haitian Anthology.* Princeton, NJ: Markus Wiener Publishing, 1999.

Bell, Martin Smartt. *All Souls' Rising* (2004); *Master of the Crossroads* (2004); *The Stone that The Builder Refused* (2006) (Haitian Revolutionary trilogy) New York City: Vintage Publishers.

Buss, Terry F., and Adam Gardner. *Haiti in the Balance: Why Foreign Aid Has Failed and What We Can Do About It.* Washington, DC: Brookings Institute Press, 2008.

Catanese, Anthony V. *Haitians: Migration and Diaspora.* Boulder, CO: Westview Press, 1999.

Constantino, Donald. *The Sacred Arts of Haitian Vodou.* Los Angeles: UCLA Fowler Museum, 1995.

Danticat, Edwidge. *Breath, Eyes, Memory* (2003); *Krik? Krak!* (2004); *The Farming of Bones* (2003). New York City: Soho Press.

———— *Brother, I'm Dying.* New York: Alfred A. Knopf, 2007.

Dash, J. Michael. *Culture & Customs of Haiti.*

———— *Literature & Ideology in Haiti (1915–1961)* Wesport, CT: Greenwood Press, 2001

———— *Haiti and the United States: National Stereotypes & the Literary Imagination*

Dayan, Joan. *Haiti, History and the Gods.* Berkeley: University of California Press, 1995.

Desmangles, Leslie. *Faces of the Gods: Vodou and Roman Catholicism in Haiti.* Chapel Hill, NC: University of North Carolina Press, 1992.

Farmer, Paul. *Aids and Accusation: Haiti and the Geography of Blame.* Los Angeles: UCLA Press, 1992.

Freeman, Bryant, and Jowel Laguerre. *Haitian Creole-English Dictionary.* Lawrence, KS: University of Kansas: Institute of Haitian Studies, 1996.

Girard, Philippe R. *Paradise Lost: Haiti's Tumultuous Journey from Pearl of the Caribbean to Third World Hot Spot.* New York City: Palgrave Macmillan, 2005.

Kidder, Tracy. *Mountains Beyond Mountains: The Quest of Dr. Paul Farmer, a Man Who Would Cure the World.* New York City: Random House, 2003.

Laguerre, Michel. *Diasporic Citizenship: Haitian Americans in Transnational America.* New York City: St. Martin's Press, 1998.

Michel, Claudine, and Patrick Bellegarde Smith (editor). *Haitian Vodou: Spirit, Myth and Reality.* Bloomington, IN: Indiana University Press, 2006.

Phipps-Kettlewell, Marilène. *Crossroads and Unholy Waters.* Carbondale, IL: Southern Illinois University Press, 2000.

Renda, Mary. *Taking Haiti: Military Occupation and the Culture of U.S. Imperialism, 1915–1940*. Chapel Hill, NC: University North Carolina Press, 2001.

Shacochis, Bob. *The Immaculate Invasion*. New York City: Penguin reprinted edition: 2000.

Schwartz, Timothy T. *Travesty in Haiti: A true Account of Christian Missions, Orphanages, Fraud, Food Aid and Drug Trafficking*. Charleston, SC: BookSurge Publishing, 2008.

White, Ashli. *Encountering Revolution: Haiti and the Making of the Early Republic (Early America: History, Context and Culture)*. Baltimore: Johns Hopkins University Press, 2010.

Zacaïr, Philippe (editor). *Haiti and the Haitian Diaspora in the Wider Caribbean*. Gainesville, FL: University Press of Florida, 2010.

About the Authors

Cécile Accilien, Ph.D.

Dr. Cécile Accilien is Associate Professor of French and Francophone literatures at Columbus State University, in Columbus, Georgia. Her primary areas of interest are Francophone Caribbean and West African literatures and films. She is the author of *Rethinking Marriage in Francophone African and Caribbean Literatures* (Lexington Books, 2008). She has also co-edited and contributed to two collections of essays, *Revolutionary Freedoms: A History of Survival, Strength and Imagination in Haiti* (Caribbean Studies Press, 2006) and *Just Below South: Intercultural Performance in the Caribbean and the U.S. South* (University of Virginia Press, 2007). She recently published an article, "Congratulations! You Don't *Look* Haitian: How and When Does One *Look* Haitian?" in *Haiti and the Haitian Diaspora in the Wider Caribbean*, edited by Philippe Zacaïr (University Press of Florida, 2010). She has been teaching French language and Francophone cultures as well as Haitian Creole since 1997.

Jowel C. Laguerre, Ph.D.

Dr. Jowel Laguerre has been the Superintendent/President of Solano Community College District (SCCD) since July 2009. Since 1978, he has taught English as a second language, French, Haitian Creole, physics, and mathematics. He published, in cooperation with Bryant C. Freeman, *Haitian Creole-English Dictionary* (Institute of Haitian Studies, Lawrence, Kansas, 2002.) Dr. Laguerre holds a Ph.D. in educational leadership (higher education), an M.S.Ed. in school administration, and an M.A. in French literature from the University of Kansas. He holds a B.A. in mathematics and physics education from L'Université d'Etat d'Haiti: Ecole Normale Supérieure, in Port-au-Prince, Haiti, and certification in teaching mathematics and French in the United States.